SHANTYTOWN PROTEST
IN PINOCHET'S CHILE

Shantytown Protest in Pinochet's Chile

CATHY LISA SCHNEIDER

Temple University Press —— Philadelphia

Temple University Press, Philadelphia 19122
Copyright © 1995 by Cathy Lisa Schneider
All rights reserved
Published 1995
Printed in the United States of America

Text designed by Judith Martin Waterman

LIBRARY OF CONGRESS CATALOGING-IN-PUBLICATION DATA
Schneider, Cathy Lisa, 1955–
    Shantytown protest in Pinochet's Chile / Cathy Lisa Schneider.
      p. cm.
    Includes bibliographical references and index.
    ISBN 1-56639-305-1 (CLOTH). — ISBN 1-56639-306-x (PAPER)
    1. Urban poor—Chile—Santiago—Political activity. 2. Urban
poor—Chile—Santiago—Political activity—Interviews. 3. Social
movements—Chile—Santiago. 4. Protest movements—Chile—
Santiago. 5. Democracy—Chile. 6. Chile—Politics and government—1973–1988. 7. Chile—History—1973–1988. I. Title.
HV4076.S26S36 1995
322.4'4'098331509047—dc20
                                                   95–2098
                                                      CIP

This book is dedicated to the memory of Rodrigo Rojas DeNegri and Miguel Leal González, who lost their lives fighting for democracy, and to Carmen Gloria Quintana and Verónica DeNegri, who survived them.

It is also dedicated to the memory of Manuel Maldonado who died fighting against AIDS in Brooklyn, New York.

And lastly, it is dedicated to the memory of my father, Nathan Schneider, who fought for a more just world and taught me to love city streets, politics, poetry, and music. Nathan passed away while I was conducting field research in Chile.

Considering our weakness
you made laws to enslave us.

In the future the laws won't be
complied with,
Considering that we don't want
to continue being slaves.

Considering that you
threaten us with guns and canons,
we remember to fear,
more than death,
the bitter life you have brought us.

—BERTOLT BRECHT
WRITTEN ON A SHANTYTOWN WALL.

CONTENTS

ILLUSTRATIONS

The research for this book began in 1975, while I was visiting a Chilean friend I had known as a first-year college student. The visit left an indelible impression. Chile in 1975 was a country in which fear penetrated one's pores. I returned to the United States that year, but my life continued to revolve around Chile.

It wasn't until June 1983, less than a month after the first national protest, that I returned to Chile, for a three month predissertation trip. Instinctively, I began to write about the protest movement. In August 1985 I resettled in a lower-middle class población in the southern zone of Santiago. To avoid endangering underground activists, I limited my study to the coding of newspaper clippings collected by the Vicaría de Solidaridad.

I also participated in monthly protests against the regime. On May 20, 1986 I was dancing a circular protest dance with a group of students on a bridge near the University of Chile law school when soldiers who had blocked our passage turned their guns and began shooting. A young medical student fell dead. Less than two months later, my friend Rodrigo Rojas De Negri was set on fire by a military patrol. He died after five days in an emergency-care center. He had been refused admission to the hospital. On September 4, another friend, Miguel Angel Leal González, was shot dead. Three days later a failed assassination attempt against General Pinochet precipitated a state of siege and four midnight-revenge murders within a week.

By mid-September I was embroiled in the movement. I was also convinced that the time needed to enter the newspaper data into a computer would be better spent in the poblaciones. According to my data, most protests had taken place in eleven or twelve "combative" poblaciones. Each of these poblaciones, I soon discovered, had been founded by the Chilean Communist Party. I asked my friends in the movement (in the underground political parties and their shantytown organizations and in human rights groups, such as the Chilean Commission of Human Rights and the Vicaria) to accompany me to these and other less combative poblaciones and introduce me to grassroots shantytown activists.

Around this time, I moved to a very poor población (Las Parcelas) on a mountain top in the eastern zone of Santiago. I also began participating in popular organizations in Yungay, La Victoria, Herminda de la Victoria, Sara Gajardo, and Remodelación. I selected, for paired structured comparisons, ten poblaciones that were similar socioeconomically and geographically (often bordering on one another), but that had been founded by different political parties. What, I asked, had been the impact of the political parties on the culture and structure of the neighborhoods? How had the distinctive relationship between neighborhoods and political parties affected levels of mobilization during authoritarian rule? In each población I interviewed the local leaders of church groups, popular economic organizations, underground parties (Left Christians, Miristas, Communists, and Socialists) and Christian Democrats. I also spoke with the local clergy and some of the less political residents of each neighborhood. All of the interviews conducted during this period, September 1986 to February 1987, were conducted under a state of siege. For this reason, I have used only first names in this book and, in many cases, those names are aliases.

I returned to Chile twice during the transition period, for two months in 1988 and six months in 1989. I also visited Chile three times during the first years of democratic rule 1990, 1991, and 1992. This book is based on interviews conducted on each of these trips and contains excerpts from those interviews, which I have translated from Spanish.

I am deeply indebted to the Chileans who entrusted their lives to my discretion. Among those whose full names I never learned or have since forgotten I want to thank Alberto and the rest of the grupo folklórico Aymara; Alonso and Dario in Las Parcelas; Chino in Granadilla; Jorge, Richard, and the Christian-based community in Sara Gajardo; Mari and the women of the Taller de Mujeres in La Granja; and the Cultural Center of Joao Goulart. Of those whose names I will always remember I wish to thank Father José Aldunate, Irma and her son Roberto Bastias, Leopoldo Benavides (both father and son), Sandra Caro, Hernán Cabrolier, José Cademártori, Guillermo Crobari, Francisco Delgado, Emilio Gautier, Raul González, Carlos Gutiérrez, José Hidalgo, Father Liam Hollahan, Violeta Ortíz Ibarra, Miguel Lawner, Marta Madrid, Francisco Martínez, Father Ronaldo Muñoz, Oscar Negrete, Pepe Ormeño, Marina Paiva, Gabriel Romero, Vicki Guajardo Roma, Gonzalo

Rovira, Augusto Samaniego, Ana Scocia, Francisco Somoza, Carola Sáez, Fabiola Sáez, Oscar Sáez, Soledad Sáez, and Patricia Torres. My time in Chile would have been much more difficult without the aid and support of Ana Arancibia, Ruth and Manuel Basoalto, Verónica Concha, Humberto Cáceres, Alamiro González, Rainer Haacke, Iván Huerta, Carmen Gloria Quintana and her family, Javier Sáez and Patricia Mansilla, María Pia de Silva, Bernardo Tapia, Ana Váldez, and Orlando Zepeda, all of whose insights helped shape this book. Thanks also go to a coterie of gringo companions, Johnny Gogan (from Ireland), Andy Daitsman, Julie Eisenberg, Carol King, and Tomas O'Keefe. Special recognition is due Enrique Kirberg and Samuel Chavkin, both of whom encouraged me throughout this project and died before its fruition. I'd also like to thank Leopoldo Benavides, Sergio Rojas, and Eduardo Morales at Facultad Latinoamericana de Ciencias Sociales; Gabriel Salazar and Alvaro Díaz at Sur Profesionales; Juan Guillermo Espinosa at the Universidad de Academia de Humanismo Cristianos; Hugo Frühling at Centro de Estudios del Desarrollo; Mario Garces at Educación y Comunicaciones; Guillermo Campero at Instituto Latinoamericana de Estudios Transnacionales; and Fernando Leiva at Promoción Intercambio de Recursos Educacionales y Tecnológicos for generously giving their time and sharing their research. Manuel Antonio Garretón and Steve Anderson helped get me out of a Chilean prison in 1989 (I was arrested upon arrival at the Santiago airport), for which I am deeply grateful. Ambassador Harry Barnes, Congressman Benjamin Gilman, and Professor George Kahin at Cornell University intervened several times to help me and, more importantly, several Chilean friends who were detained, "disappeared," or in danger. In the

United States, Alejandro and Eliana Parra, Cecilia and Leonardo Vargas, Verónica DeNegri, Nieves Ayres and Victor Torres, Margarie and Rosamel Millaman, Marta and Ricardo Olivares, and Edmundo Torneria provided me friendship and a continuous connection to Chile.

This book owes a great debt to Cornell University and my doctoral dissertation committee Eldon Kenworthy, Sidney Tarrow, and Benedict O. Anderson. Eldon Kenworthy was a supportive and encouraging dissertation chair, with an unwavering commitment to Latin America. Benedict Anderson's knowledge of military regimes, both intellectual and personal, and his commitment to Indonesia during and after the military coup, inspired me during some of my worst periods in Chile. Sidney Tarrow was the book's most important intellectual influence. His brilliant analysis of social movements and of European Communist parties put my Chilean work into a broader theoretical framework. His insightful comments, on both the dissertation and, later, the book manuscript, were invaluable. Charles Tilly read the book manuscript three times and made incisive comments each time. He has been a great inspiration, and I value his friendship. Alejandro Portes and Peter Winn's books and articles on pre-coup Chile provided a historical context for my work. They both read the manuscript and gave me valuable advice. The Latin American Studies Center at Cornell, the Social Science faculty at St. Lawrence University, and both the Watson Institute and Comparative Development Studies Center at Brown University provided funding for several trips to Chile. Marc Chernick offered me an office and companionship at Columbia University. Vivienne Bennett, Susan Borenstin, Louise Jezierski, Doug McAdam, Jim Morone, Eric Nordlinger, David Ost, Julia

Paley, and Dietrich Rueshmeyer all read parts of the book manuscript and gave me useful feedback.

Parts of this book were published in article form as "Mobilization at the Grassroots: Shantytown Resistance in Authoritarian Chile" in the Winter 1991 issue of *Latin American Perspectives*, and I am grateful to the issue editor, Lois Oppenheim, and to Kemy Oyarzun who requested its submission. Arturo Escobar and Sonia Alvarez published a revised version as "Radical Opposition Parties and Squatters Movements in Pinochet's Chile," in *The Making of Social Movements in Latin America: Identity, Strategy and Democracy* in 1992. Both are dear friends and have provided intellectual stimulation and support. Gabriel Salazar published a version of the article in Chile, as "La movilización de las bases: Poblaciones marginales y resistencia en Chile autoritario," which his daughter translated into Spanish. The North American Congress on Latin America (NACLA) published part of an early version of chapter six, as "Chile: The Underside of the Miracle" in *A Market Solution for the Americas: The Rise of Wealth and Hunger* (26, no. 4, February). NACLA Editor Fred Rosen, Associate Editor Diedre McFaddyen, and Director Pierre La Ramee and his partner, my friend, Erica Polokoff, have all been helpful.

I was fortunate to have two great book reviewers, who decided not to remain anonymous. Thank you Steven Volk and Howard Winant. Steven Volk read the manuscript twice and provided detailed comments both times. He also introduced me to Jill Hamburg, who generously gave me all her material on poblaciones in pre-coup Chile. Special thanks go to my copy editor, Judith Martin Waterman, my acquisitions editor, Doris Braendel, and the other members of the editorial board at Temple University Press. My research assistant at American University, Jennifer Nadeau, drew the map of Santiago, helped copy edit the manuscript, and provided the index. I am grateful for all of their careful and painstaking efforts.

I also wish to thank the Aaron Diamond Foundation for supporting my study of neighborhood organizing in New York City from 1993–1996. The work in New York constantly shed new light on my work in Chile. Particular thanks go to Musica against Drugs founders Manny Maldonado, Belen Reyes, and Chris Lanier and to outreach directors, Ruben Bonilla and Augie Rivera. Also thanks to Alan Clear and Raquel Algarin at Lower East Side Harm Reduction Center, Joyce Rivera Beckman, Edwin Santiago, and Philip Pinckney at St. Ann's Corner of Harm Reduction, and Angelo Falcon at the Institute of Puerto Rican Policy.

I am especially grateful to my students (particularly Amy Coughenour, Tamar Dolgen, Alicia Korton, Ramon González, David Maizlish, Rachel Sherman, Stacy Shwartz, and Peter Young) for their enthusiasm; my friends (in addition to those mentioned above, Frances Adams, Peter Andreas, Maureen Barry-Grande, Alan Cafruny, Robin Weiss Castro, Maria Lorena Cook, Greg DeLaurier, Farhat Haq, J. J. Johnson, Geoff Levy, Phil and Miriam Mauceri, Jim Morrell, Peter and Angela Nastasi, Manny and Christine Resto, and Carina Sinclair) and my colleagues at American University for their encouragement; my mother Frieda Schneider, for her patience, sustenance and humor; my brothers David Schneider and Steven VanDresser, my sister Lauren Simchi, and my nieces and nephews (Chana, Eyal, Yehuda, Naomi, Moshe Noah, Malka (Molly), Yeshua Aaron, and Batya Esther) for their love and enduring faith.

ACRONYMS

ACU	Agrupación Cultural Universitaria; University Cultural Association
AD	Alianza Democrática; Democratic Alliance
ARCO	Asamblea de Renovación Comunista; Assembly of Communist Renovation
AVEC	Agrupación Vecinal; Association of Neighbors
CEPCH	Confederación de Empleados Particulares de Chile; Union of White-Collar Employees
CLAT	Confederación Latinoamericana de Trabajadores; Latin American Confederation of Workers
CNI	Central Nacional de Información; National Center of Information
CNS	Coordinador Nacional Sindical; National Union Coordinator
CNT	Comando Nacional de Trabajadores; Command of National Workers
COAPO	Coordinadora de Agrupación Poblacionales; Coordinator of Popular Associations

CODEM	Comité de Defensa de Derechos de Mujer; Committee in Defense of the Rights of Women
COPACHI	Comité de Cooperación para la Paz en Chile; Committee of Cooperation for Peace in Chile
CORA	Corporación de Reforma Agraria; Corporation of Land Reform
CORHABIT	Caja de Habitación; Housing Authority
CORVI	Corporación de Vivienda; Housing Corporation
CTC	Confederación de Cobre; Copper Confederation
CUP	Comando Unitario Poblacional; United Shantytown Command
CUT	Central Única de Trabajadores; Central Union of Workers
DC	Demócrata Cristianos; Christian Democrats
DIFA	Dirección de Inteligencia de la Fuerza Aérea
DINA	Dirección Nacional de Inteligencia; Directorate of National Intelligence
FECECH	Federación de Centros de Estudiantes de Chile; Federation of Centers of Students at the University of Chile
FECH	Federación de Estudiantes de Universidad de Chile; Federation of Students of the University of Chile

FEUC	Federación de Estudiantes de Universidad Católica; Federation of Students of Catholic University
FLN	Frente de Liberación Nacional; National Liberation Front
FOch	Federación Obrera de Chile; Workers Federation of Chile
FPMR	Frente Patriótico Manuel Rodríguez; Manuel Rodríguez Patriotic Front
FRAP	Frente de Acción Popular; Popular Action Front
FUT	Frente Unitario Trabajador; United Workers' Front
MAPU	Movimiento de Acción Popular Unitaria; Popular Action Movement
MDP	Movimiento Democrático Popular; Democratic Popular Movement
MEMCH	Movimiento pro Emancipación de la Mujer; Movement for Women's Emancipation
MIR	Movimiento de la Izquierda Revolucionaria; Movement of the Revolutionary Left
MUDECHI	Mujeres de Chile; Women of Chile
PAL	Partido de Agricultura Laboral; Agrarian Labor Party
PC or PCch	Partido Comunista or Partido Comunista de Chile; Communist Party or Chilean Communist Party

PEM	Programa de Empleo Mínimo; Minimal Employment Program
PIDE	Partido de Izquierda Independiente; Party of the Independent Left
PN	Partido Nacional; Nationalist Party
POJH	Programa Ocupacional para Jefes de Hogar; Occupational Program for Heads of Household
POS	Partido Obrero Socialista; Socialist Workers Party
PPD	Partido para la Democracia; Party for Democracy
PR	Partido Radical; Radical Party
PS	Partido Socialista; Socialist Party
PSP	Partido Socialista Popular; Popular Socialist Party
SICAR	Servicio Inteligencia de Carabineros; Police Intelligence Service
SIFA	Servicio de Inteligencia de Fuerza Aérea; Air force Intelligence Service
SIN	Servicio de Inteligencia Naval; Naval Intelligence Service
UNTRACH	Unión Nacional de Trabajadores Chilenos; National Union of Chilean Workers
UP	Unidad Popular; Popular Unity

SHANTYTOWN PROTEST IN
PINOCHET'S CHILE

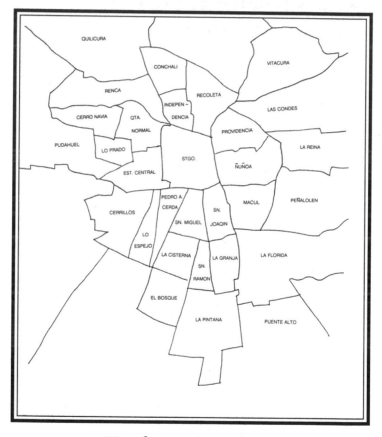

Map of greater Santiago, 1990

CHAPTER ONE

Introduction

The Coup

On a cold grey September morning, in 1973, the Chilean armed forces attacked the presidential palace of democratically elected Marxist president Salvador Allende. Within hours the palace was in flames, the president dead, and leading members of the government imprisoned or in hiding. Before the flames were extinguished, tanks and helicopters assaulted Santiago's impoverished *poblaciones* (urban slums and shantytowns) forcing tens of thousands of Chileans from their homes.

For the residents of Santiago's slums and shantytowns September 11 was a shattering experience. As one resident observed, "in a single day, a lifetime of work and dreams was torn asunder in a campaign of random violence and terror." But the children growing up in Santiago's "belts of misery" were even more deeply affected, and their trauma at the time of the coup lead inexorably to their activism in later decades.

When Gabriel was nine, living in a northern Santiago shantytown, the earth itself seemed to tremble:

> We lived so close to the Moneda (presidential palace) that the ground underneath us rose and fell with each assault. My mother said "war has come." We began to burn everything in the house, books, photos, newspapers. Before the military evacuated the area they had arrested both my father and brother. They later released my father, but they held my brother in a clandestine torture center for over two years.

For Alonso, thirteen at the time of the coup and living in a southern Santiago shantytown, September 11 was a day marked by murder:

> I remember the military in trucks and tanks, shooting everywhere. The children began a game. As the military advanced the children would hide in their houses, but when the military retreated the children would return to the streets. I remember I saw a truck pass, dripping blood. There was another truck standing alone, and a soldier asked me to help him. Trembling, I helped him lift a dead body into the truck. The corpse had a bullet wound in its back. I remember lifting the body as if it were a time bomb. It was my first contact with death.

September 11 was also the last day Mari, thirteen and living in the famous "red" (with heavy Communist influence) district of San Miguel, saw her father. "I don't even remember the coup, it's as if I have it blocked. All I remember is passing my father in the street. He yelled at me to quick, run home and burn everything in the house. He didn't return after that."

The experiences of Gabriel, Alonso, and Mari were not

unusual. By mid-1975 the military had detained between forty and fifty thousand civilians, brutally torturing many of them (Ad Hoc Working Group of the United Nations 1975, 50). They summarily executed, or "disappeared," over two thousand. They attacked every traditional feature of Chilean society—Congress, political parties, labor unions, neighborhood organizations, even local parishes.

For ten years, the only national institution able to defy the regime was the Catholic Church. Its increasing dedication to the struggle for human rights pushed it into direct conflict with the regime. At the local level, the church acted as an umbrella, protecting activists and victims alike. In the shantytowns, small human-rights and economic-subsistence organizations began to appear; in factories, labor organizers recreated underground political networks; and in universities, students defied regulations prohibiting political discussion and organized demonstrations against the regime. Yet these struggles all shared a common denominator; they were local, ephemeral, and easily repressed. As Alfred Stepan notes, "In Chile, eight years of authoritarian rule passed without significant movement out of the initial authoritarian situation: civil society remained debilitated in the face of state strength" (Stepan 1985, 322). The military appeared invincible. In May 1980, Augusto Pinochet held a plebiscite on a new constitution, institutionalizing his rule, and won overwhelmingly.

The Protests

Suddenly, on May 11, 1983, a storm of protest swept through Santiago's streets. The severe economic crisis of 1982 had divided military supporters, expanding political opportunities

(McAdam, 1982; Tarrow, 1989b) and opening the doors to a growing movement of opposition. And, as if a spell had been broken, unarmed students, workers, and shantytown residents flooded the streets demanding an immediate end to military rule. At the forefront of this emerging protest movement were the same poblaciones, targeted by the military for almost a decade.

In the *población* in which Alonso lived, residents built burning barricades, drummed pots and pans, and organized marches. In the poblaciones where Mari and Gabriel lived, protestors sprayed walls with political slogans, lead mass marches, and cut electricity to large portions of the city by throwing metal objects at electric cables. When the armed forces attacked these seemingly defenseless communities, residents responded by digging trenches, erecting burning barricades, and pelting military tanks with rocks. The deluge of protests in the same shantytowns that had been the target of military repression between 1973–1983 challenged the military's claim to have reshaped political loyalties in Chile. "In 1983, with the protests" Genaro Arriagada would later reflect, "Chile rediscovered the part of its reality that, in the delirium of the economic miracle, it had forgotten. From the start of those mass demonstrations, names [of poblaciones] like La Pincoya, La José María Caro, La Victoria regained their Chilean citizenship and a place among the concerns of Chileans" (cited in Timerman 1987, 70).

For three years the protests raged. On July 2 and 3, 1986, the protest cycle reached its peak with a massive nationwide strike. The military responded with a new wave of repression. Ten people were killed, raising the number of protest-related deaths to over four hundred.

By August 1986, exhaustion had set in. Shantytown residents returned to the safety of their homes. Those who

CATHY LISA SCHNEIDER

Airport reception, in September 1986, for the body of Roberto Parada, the well-known actor who fled Chile and died in exile a year after his son José Manuel Parada was tortured and then had his throat cut by the Chilean police. Estella Ortiz (José Manuel's widow and Communist Party candidate for deputy in 1989) is on the far left; her father was also disappeared by the regime. María Maluanda (Roberto's widow and José Manuel's mother, currently a senator for the Party for Democracy) is in the center. Ramiro Olivares (a doctor and Amnesty International Prisoner of Conscience who served a year in jail for having treated a boy with a bullet wound before informing the military) is on the right.

continued to resist the dictatorship through direct confrontation had become isolated. By 1987, only a small minority of *pobladores* (residents of poblaciones) was either organized or active. As Gabriel notes, "in 1984, I went underground. I wanted to fight the dictatorship directly. I was not alone in this. By 1987, there was not a single Communist in my población who organized in the open."

The Christian Democratic and allied sectors of the Socialist Party abandoned the protests. In 1987, they formed a coalition for free elections. In 1988, the coalition became the basis for the Coalition for No, a broad front aimed at defeating Pinochet in the upcoming, constitutionally mandated, plebiscite. On October 11, 1988, Pinochet lost the plebiscite on his presidency. In December 1989, the regime held democratic elections, and the opposition soundly defeated Pinochet's hand-selected candidate. On March 11, 1990, a democratically elected, civilian government took office.

THIS STORY OF PROTEST AND REPRESSION raises critical questions about the nature of political life in authoritarian Chile and our theoretical understanding of social movements and revolutions. Why did impoverished and almost defenseless shantytowns emerge as the center of resistance to authoritarian rule? Why did shantytown residents risk arrest, torture, and even death to fight a regime they seemed to have so little chance of defeating? Why did protests center in some shantytowns, but not others? Why did they suddenly decline in 1986? And, lastly, to what extent and in what way did the shantytown struggle contribute to the return to democratic rule in 1990?

This book examines the Chilean transition to democracy from the bottom up. It begins at the grassroots of civil society, during the clandestine phase of the struggle, when activists began the difficult work of reconstructing the first organizations of resistance. It moves from the underground organizing of the immediate postcoup years to the open confrontations that began in 1983 when students, workers, and shantytown dwellers stormed the streets demanding the resignation of Augusto Pinochet. It ends, where most of the transition to democracy literature begins, with the 1988 plebiscite campaign, and the 1990 return to democratic rule.

This book is both an oral history, based on over a hundred interviews collected in Santiago's shantytowns between 1985–1992, and a comparative sociology that explores political differences among shantytowns in the same city. It concentrates, not on general processes and abstract structural change, but on the struggles of poor people to create and sustain organizations of resistance. It is about communities, personal networks, and shared historical memories and their power to unite individuals around a common goal. Its heroes are not political leaders, or members of the military establishment, but rather poor people who "burst through the boundaries of the accepted limits of social behavior," (Tarrow 1989b, 7) and risked their lives to fight tyranny and injustice.

This book, then, is about politics, about the context in which individuals make choices about their lives, and the political histories that shape their vision of the possible. As such, it fills an important gap in the literature on social movements. Some of these writings see protests as a spontaneous response to grievances, real or imagined. Others see them as the result of manipulation by a skilled political elite. Both approaches view protests only as they appear from outside or above. They omit history and historical continuities, leave aside the political context that determines how individuals organize around grievances, blur the distinctions between successful and unsuccessful centers of protest and, most broadly, fail to flesh out the nexus between political and civil society.

Political scientists and sociologists such as Genaro Arriagada (1988) and Eduardo Valenzuela (1984), for example, explain the eruption of protest in Santiago's shantytowns as a result of the deprivation, social dissolution, and anger produced by the 1982 economic crisis. "During the protest years the poblaciones consisted of a mass of unorganized individuals and a few isolated, weak and unfinanced organizations of several thousand residents" (Arriagada 1988, 61).

Yet, this explanation runs up against a significant set of facts. In 1983, there was no association between the level of economic depression and the intensity and scope of protest action. Those poblaciones hit hardest by the crisis, in relative or absolute terms, responded weakly to the call for protests. When protests emerged in these areas, they were short-lived, the protesters being unable to withstand the accompanying repression.

Other sociologists, including Tilman Evers (1985), Fernando Leiva and James Petras (1986), and Teresa Valdés (1987) focus on the construction of autonomous neighborhood organizations and the formation of a new social actor, the *poblador* movement, to explain the eruption of protests. Valdes, for instance, argues that the economic crisis fortified the poblador organizations, and catapulted the poblador movement into national political prominence (Valdes 1987, 296).

But those pobladores who joined soup kitchens or economic cooperatives did not necessarily participate in the protests or the so-called "poblador movement." The steady increase in the number of economic-subsistence organizations between 1983 and 1989 does not explain the irregular pattern of protest activity across both space and time. Protests did not occur with equal intensity in all poblaciones, or on all national protest days. Protests were most intense in June, July, and August of 1983, September and October of 1984, September of 1985, and July of 1986. They erupted most forcefully in the traditional Communist shantytowns. Indeed, Eugenio Tironi insists, "the so-called poblador movement has been completely confused with the activity of traditional political activists" (Tironi 1987, 74).

But the 1983–1986 poblador movement, if not the harbinger of a new social actor, or a spontaneous riposte to the 1982 economic crisis, was far more than an isolated group of political activists organizing rebellion in shantytowns. The capacity of Santiago's poor urban neighborhoods to mobilize mass political resistance, despite a decade of severe military repression, lay in the political heritage of decades of work in the popular culture and in the formation of a skilled generation of grassroots militants.

> Grassroots activists who had been active years before the coup played key leadership roles in all these organizing activities. As one party leader noted "we as parties could do little, but political activists at the local level rebuilt the social movement during the darkest moments of the regime." The ideological and political consciousness that broad sectors of the population had acquired over the years prepared them for political work at the community level and for organizing around local needs, even when their ties to the political leadership had been broken. (Burbach 1989, 18)

In Chile, the politicization, organization, and solidarity

in such shantytowns were a direct consequence of their historical ties to the Chilean Communist Party and the party's consistent emphasis on the creation of solidary communities with skilled grassroots leaders. Much as the left-wing enclaves of the American civil-rights movement, "these enclaves of elders and subterranean channels, rivulets, deep-running springs . . . [nurtured] unconventional wisdom, moods, and mystiques. With left wing politics in a state of collapse most of these opposition spaces were cultural—ways of living, thinking, and fighting oneself free of the . . . consensus" (Gitlin 1987, 28).

Those who became politicized because of contact with the Communist Party or Communist neighborhoods—even those who became militants of other political parties or never joined a political party at all—shared a political conception: they identified their problems in structural terms, and sought solutions through collective action. Life in traditional Communist neighborhoods overcame a fundamental attribution error—the tendency of people to explain their situation as a function of individual, rather than situational, factors (McAdam, 1982). As one Christian Democrat living in a Communist población explained, "I used to be ashamed of my poverty, I saw it as a personal failure. A Communist neighborhood organizer explained to me that I needn't be ashamed. That we all shared the same problems."

"Revolutionary culture is the product of politics." It is through the conscious strategies of political parties that "communities, real or imagined . . . become active agents" of change (C. Smith 1990, 271). In Chile, decades of political struggle had convinced residents of Communist directed shantytowns that their fate was inextricably linked to that of their community and that solidary collective activity was capable of defeating even the most powerful regime.

THE EXPERIENCES OF ALONSO, GABRIEL, AND MARI, three of the leaders of the shantytown movement interviewed for this study, are illustrative. All three learned their organizational skills in Communist shantytowns. Alonso began organizing in the Communist shantytown Yungay because he felt isolated in the shantytown where he lived. "In my población, people were afraid to participate, and they were ashamed of their poverty. They were always worried about appearances." Status and occupational differences were exacerbated by political conflicts and distrust. "They called us extremists, politicos," recalls Alonso. "In Yungay the neighbors had a different attitude. They said, "Look at my house! How dare they force us to live in such misery." Their sense of shared suffering empowered them and encouraged them to work for collective solutions. "People who are in similar situations and who have identical interests often find themselves in competition with one another . . . the relative salience of class [as a collective identity] . . . is a cumulative consequence of strategies pursued by parties of the left" (Przeworski, 1985).

Even Gabriel, who was traumatized by the coup, only became politically aware when he moved to the Communist shantytown Herminda de la Victoria:

> After the disappearance of my brother, my whole family was badly traumatized, but we blocked it in a sort of collective amnesia. I remember my mother and I, three years later, applauding Pinochet!
>
> In 1977, I moved to Herminda de la Victoria with my

sister. Herminda changed my life. I began to understand what was going on around me. First, I became involved with the Christian community. The Church attracted me because of its devotion to the poor. I even considered becoming a priest. . . . But in the Christian community there were many members of the Communist Youth whose courage and commitment appealed to me. Indeed, of the eight of us new to the Christian community, five would later join the Communist Youth.

For Mari, born and raised in a Communist family in the Communist población La Victoria, identification with the Communist Party was never in doubt. The Communist Party had politicized the neighborhood so successfully that the other political parties also found it easier to organize in La Victoria. As Hugo Flores, president of Solidaridad (the Christian Democratic shantytown organization) observes:

> Even the priests participate in La Victoria . . . since residents are more conscious of their role in the struggle. La Legua, as well, like Cerro Navia and La Pincoya [are three other poblaciones that, like La Victoria, are Communist and mobilized]" (interview with Hugo Flores in Santiago, December 1989).

The Reemergence of Political Parties

During the first ten years of the dictatorship, these informal grassroots networks were the only resources available to the urban poor. Informal networks linked political activists to one another, gave movement members a sense of community and identity, and reinforced their faith in both the power of collective action and the importance of their own contribution to such action. In 1983, a national economic crisis created the political context for the reemergence of formal political parties, unions, and nongovernmental organizations. These institutions provided neighborhood organizers with new resources, such as meeting halls, salaries, and national support networks, inspiring an explosion of grassroots activity, even in the less organized poblaciones. But the reemergence of political parties also damaged the movement in several respects.

First, political infighting alienated some pobladores thereby reducing political participation. As one organizer recalls, "We were so busy trying to control the organizations that we didn't notice that once we controlled them, everyone else abandoned them."

Second, political divisions and conflicts over strategy and tactics confused Santiago residents. On September 4, 1986, there were four separate calls for political action ranging from the Christian Democratic plea for a day of prayer and silence, to the Movemento de la Izquierda Revolucionaria's (MIR; Movement of the Revolutionary Left—a guerilla group formed by Universidad de Concepción students in 1967) cry for an indefinitely prolonged general strike.

Third, the 1980 decision of the Communist Party leadership (living in exile in the then U.S.S.R.) to pursue an insurrectional strategy isolated its members from other shantytown residents. While the focus of Communist activists before 1983, was on rebuilding social organizations and linking people who shared grievances, after 1983, the Communist Party began to pull its leaders out of mass organizations and employ them in clandestine military operations.

In so doing it brought down a rain of repression on the poblaciones in which the Party once had been most welcome.

Fourth, the reemergence of the more moderate parties provided movement leaders with whom the government could negotiate, and, thus, drive a wedge between them and the more radical shantytown activists. The more moderate movement leaders were gradually reabsorbed into normal political channels, while the shantytown activists were isolated, repressed, and demobilized. Ironically, it was the government's concessions to these moderates that created the conditions for Pinochet's defeat in the 1988 plebiscite and Chile's return to democratic rule. The transition to democracy was simply the final phase of the protest cycle.

The Chilean protest movement followed a pattern similar to that of other successful protest movements in the East and West (Shorter and Tilly 1974; McAdam 1982; Pizzorno 1978; Castells 1983; Tarrow 1989b; Eisenstadt 1992). Like the American civil-rights movement, it began in traditionally active grassroots communities where solid communication networks, solidary incentives, and an established infrastructure linked "members of an aggrieved population," and recruited "activists by virtue of their involvement in [previous] organizations" (McAdam 1982, 43–48). These neighborhoods functioned like a "small motor that later turned the larger motor of the mass movement" (Gitlin 1987, 26).

Like the French strike waves of the 1960s, the scale and intensity of protest depended closely on "the prior organization of workers in the setting, on the availability of a structure that identifies, accumulates, and communicates grievances on the one hand, and facilitates collective action on the other" (Shorter and Tilly 1974, 81). Its leaders were like those of the 1970s citizens' movement in Spain, "fully political: they introduced political goals and consciousness into the movement and connected it to leftist politics in the broadest sense . . . [yet] they were able to develop a widely supported network because they focused primarily on urban issues" (Castells 1983).

Political parties and unions mobilized in Chile, as they did in the prodemocracy movements in Eastern Europe and the Soviet Union, around alternative collective identities and "conceptions of the good" (Eisenstadt, 1992). These identities, solidarities, and commitments were "forged— shaped, destroyed, and molded anew—as the political parties . . . strive[d] to impose on the masses a particular vision of society" (Przeworski, 1985).

The Chilean movement also followed a cyclical pattern, similar to that observed by Pizzorno and Tarrow in their studies of protests in France and Italy (Pizzorno 1978; Tarrow 1989b). The cycle was forged through the interaction of formal (political parties and institutions) and informal (political culture, collective identities, and solidarity networks) political resources. The movement began in communities where political parties had formed strong collective identities and solidary bonds. An economic crisis allowed organizers to draw new adherents, to extend the movement's scope, and to mobilize widespread resistance. Political parties returned and were thrust into prominence. Competition for control of the movement brought a stream of resources (salaries, meeting halls, concert artists, media support) to the shantytowns, infusing the movement with new energy. Simultaneously, the return of formal political parties, and their attempts to gain control over the new movement, weakened informal solidary networks. As confrontations with the state became more violent and costly, moderate political leaders adopted a conciliatory stance, winning significant concessions from the state. The movement declined as the party elites cut the flow of political resources to grassroots activists.

It is from this "political process" perspective that we can best understand the Chilean movement. Like more institutional forms of political action, it emerged from within the confines of traditional political alignments, and was shaped by traditional political actors and institutions, in particular the popular culture that was the heritage of the Chilean Communist Party. At the same time, the movement was transformative. It introduced new political actors, established new repertoires of collective action, and paved the way for the reemergence of Chilean democracy. It also recast the contours of Chilean political life.

CHAPTER TWO

The Making of the Chilean Left

The literature on urban poverty is as myriad as that on social movements. Most studies, however, fall within three analytic categories. The first are the social-psychological theories drawn largely from Durkheim. According to them, the urban poor do not share sufficiently the norms of mainstream society. Their marginal connection to political and economic institutions predisposes them toward violence and criminal activity. While the first generation of urban poor retains links to the norms and structures of rural life, and thus a tendency to be apolitical and passive, those born in the city are predisposed toward riots and revolution. Huntington argues, for instance, that the rural migrant "brings with him rural values and attitudes, including well-established behavior patterns of social deference and political passivity. A low level of political consciousness and political information pervades the urban slums" (Huntington 1968, 279). But those born in the city "are likely to be swept by social violence, as the children of the city demand the rewards of the city. . . . In Asia, Africa, and Latin America urban violence, political and criminal is due to rise as the proportion of natives to immigrants in the city rises" (Huntington 1968, 280).

Proponents of the rational-actor model suggest an alternate theory of violence. They argue that the poor are neither irrational nor prone to ideological politics. As Janice Perlman puts it, they are pragmatic and act in a way that is rational given the difficult situation they confront; they try to "maximize favors from the political system and minimize loss" (Perlman 1976, 127). Shantytown dwellers display a "keen understanding of the existing reality" and a sensible concern "with those issues that affect their lives most directly and wisely disrupt the system least. . . . The very recognition of their vulnerability is itself a sign of . . . political astuteness and pragmatism" (Perlman 1976, 173–187).

The third approach focuses on political culture and political socialization. This category includes the work of Alejandro Portes, Daniel Goldrich, Charles Tilly, Sidney Tarrow, and Manuel Castells. These theorists reject homogeneous descriptions of the poor. They argue that the character of a neighborhood depends not only on its socioeconomic status, but also on the intersection of political institutions, social movements, and urban geography. Variations in timing, terms of incorporation, and group capacities establish distinctive types of linkage between groups and the policy arenas. These linkages have logical consequences for the process of group formation, for the character of policy demands the groups will make, and for the content of the policy arena (Tilly and Tilly 1975). The linkages between political parties and the poor decide the political culture and ideology of urban neighborhoods. As

Robert Putnam argues, formal institutions can produce informal changes that become self-sustaining (Putnam 1993, 184). Some poor neighborhoods will reflect high degrees of social organization, while others will remain disorganized and fragmented.

This book is deeply indebted to the third group of theorists. It argues that the rings of poverty surrounding the center of Santiago were like the rings of many Latin American cities, made up of hundreds of separate and distinct communities. The communities in the farthest outskirts were poorly organized, and residents displayed little propensity for political action. In other districts, however, communities such as La Victoria in the red district of San Miguel, or Yungay in La Granja, or Herminda de la Victoria in Cerro Navia, residents were well organized and politically sophisticated. Communist "socialization taught this impoverished population to reinterpret their personal travails in new ways that placed blame on the dominant social structure rather than self" (Portes 1993). When successful, this "strategy produced individuals who were not only politically active, but also militantly opposed to the existing order and willing to make more radical demands on behalf of the poor" (Portes 1976, 105).

The diversity of Chile's urban slums, then, and the strong organization and politicization of particular neighborhoods were a consequence of their intimate relationship to the political parties. This relationship was a product of 1. the dependence of the Chilean economy on mining exports from northern desert enclaves; 2. the early emergence of a national labor movement and national labor parties under Marxist leadership, preceding universal suffrage by five decades; 3. the impetus, created by wars, economic depressions and import substitution policies, for the migration of thousands of skilled, left-wing activists to the capital city; and 4. "the extension of urban space in Santiago by means of politically directed, collectively organized land invasions" (Klaarhamer 1989, 177). This bond between neighborhoods and parties was cemented through waves of political mobilization that "had created a vast and rich net of voluntary associations [and] pressure groups . . . whose established loyalties were difficult to manipulate or break" (Huneus 1987a, 10, see also Waugh 1992, 7).

The Origins of Marxism in Chile

Chile's Marxist parties trace their beginnings to the struggles in the nitrate mines in the late nineteenth century. Chile's northern enclave economy, with its center in isolated desert terrain, taught workers to "reject unsatisfactory conditions, . . . defy authority, . . . and trust themselves, their friends, and their relatives in their search for a better life. . . . Through creative and often experimental activities, nitrate workers developed—however incompletely and imperfectly—autonomous tools of organization and socialization that cracked the cultural monopoly of the Chilean ruling class" (Bergquist 1986, 52–54).

In the 1880s, *mancomunals*, or mutual aid societies, provided mine workers in the isolated northern nitrate territory with support services, such as health care, unemployment insurance, and disability pay and cultural services such as newspapers, theater groups, and sports clubs. By 1890 the mancomunals had initiated a series of strikes, which spread rapidly throughout the region. "By the time the military brought the situation under control an estimated ten to fifteen nitrate workers had been killed and about a hundred wounded. The strike wave spread south from Tarapacá, reached as far as the coal fields of Lota and Coronel, and touched all the major industrial and port centers in between" (J. Morris 1966, 97–98).

By the end of the decade over ten thousand workers had participated in over three hundred strikes. Chile's urban centers and industrial working classes had also grown. Santiago and Valparaiso, in particular, had become centers of trade and commerce. In both cities, geographical inequalities accentuated economic inequalities, as the rich lived together in the center of the city, surrounded by concentric rings of poverty. Wealth and status were reflected in proximity to the city center.

> The traditional Latin American city reflected the homogeneity of its social structure. Centers of political and religious authority were located in the main "plaza de armas," in turn surrounded by the homes of the most prominent families: these were followed by houses of middle-level merchants and professionals, which eventually gave way to artisan shops and dwellings; finally the urban periphery was occupied by the most humble sectors, day servants and an incipient proletariat of unskilled laborers. The social ranking of the family was in rough correspondence to the distance form the main plaza. . . . The homogeneity and unidimensionality that this ecology reflected were only to be definitely broken with the massive movements of internal migration well within the last century (Portes 1971, 698–699).

As Santiago grew, so did the urban tenements of its

outer rings. By 1910, over 25 percent of Santiago's population, or one hundred thousand people, lived in twenty-five thousand one-room dwellings without private cooking facilities or toilets. Most lacked windows or any source of ventilation (Vial 1981, 878). In the early 1900s, about 97 percent of workers lived in this type of inadequate housing (V. Espinosa 1988, 54). Many of the earliest workers' strikes involved issues of housing and rent.

By 1902 the labor movement had spread throughout Chile, and with it industrial unrest. Between 1902 and 1907, there were over two hundred workers' strikes in Chile's major cities, with eighty in 1907 alone. They include,

> the 1903 dock strike in Valparaiso, in which 40 workers were killed; the "red week" in Santiago in 1905, during which protesters virtually seized control of Santiago for several days and which left 200 to 400 dead or wounded; [and] the 1906 railway workers' strike in Antofagasta in which 150 workers may have been killed (Collier and Collier 1991, 73; see also J. O. Morris 1966, 98–99; Barría 1971, 19; Angell 1972, 13).

The strike wave culminated in Iquique in 1907, when mine owners called for state support to quash the rebellion. In the process, between one and three thousand unarmed workers, wives, and children, were slaughtered (Collier and Collier 1991, 73).

The ferocity of the repression in Iquique radicalized the union movement. "The single document prepared by a worker's organization published in the Parliamentary Commission's report of 1913 declared that five minutes of officially sanctioned gunfire had done more to destroy their patriotism and respect for government authority than 'a half century of systematic propaganda by a thousand anarchists'" (Bergquist 1986, 56).

The repression also forced labor to retreat. Strike activity declined, and the "Democratic Party, which had been the dominant force among the mutual aid societies, began to look elsewhere for support. It moved away from a working class program as it sought to broaden its base" (Collier and Collier 1991, 74; see also J. S. Valenzuela 1979, 433). The rightward shift of the Democratic Party, in the wake of Iquique, convinced Senator Luis Emilio Recabarren of the need for a class-based, political party. He emerged as a central force behind the creation of the Partido Obrero Socialista (POS, the Socialist Workers Party) in 1912. The POS, in turn, was instrumental in the creation of the Ligas de Arrendatarios (tenants associations) in 1914, and the conversion of the conservative mutualist association Gran Federación Obrera de Chile (GFOCh, founded in 1909) into the Federación Obrera de Chile (FOCh), the Marxist, Workers Federation of Chile, in 1917.

The conversion of the conservative GFOCh into a militant, left-wing, national union federation pushed the POS into national political prominence (Barnard 1978, 44). It and other anticapitalist labor organizations multiplied in size and influence in the postwar period, spurred by the plummeting international market for nitrates and the growing economic depression.

> Socialists dominated the labor organizations in the nitrate zone, anarcho-syndicalists were preeminent in Santiago, and the Chilean chapter of the Industrial Workers of the World came to predominate in the port of Valparaiso. It was the Socialists, however, who made their strength and

influence in the national labor and political organizations.
Years of struggle in the nitrate zone had convinced socialists that a solution to the problems of the working class
would have to be a national one, achieved through access
to the state (Bergquist 1986, 61).

Despite an 1874 law extending suffrage to all literate
males over twenty-one, in 1915 less than 10 percent of the
population was eligible to vote. Without the vote, workers
could not defeat the Liberal and Conservative parties in
Congress. Without representation in Congress, workers
could not wrest economic concessions from the oligarchy
(the Liberal Party represented landowners and the church
and the Conservatives represented bankers, merchants, and
industrialists). The battle against economic exploitation
became indelibly linked to the battle for both universal
suffrage and free education.

By 1919 labor had shifted the locus of political activity
from the local to the national level. In August 100,000
protesters thronged the capital. In September general strikes
shut down Santiago, Iquique, Antofagasta, and
Chuquicamata (Collier and Collier 1991, 74; Monteon 1982,
139). Between 1917 and 1919 labor struck over 110 times
(Collier and Collier 1991, 75; DeShazo 1983, 165), and in
1920 over 50,000 workers engaged in over 105 major strikes
(Faundez 1988, 31).

The mass mobilizations inspired Arturo Alessandri's
1920 presidential campaign. Leading a Liberal Alliance coalition of Radicals, Democrats, and Liberal reformers,
Alessandri's campaign mixed elements of populism, pater-
nalism, and prudence. The more conservative members of
the Liberal Party allied themselves with the Conservative

Party in the National Union Coalition, committed to de-
fending tradition, family, and property. Neither coalition
challenged the fundamental structure of power.

> To a large extent, Alessandri and his more conservative
> opponents represented two elite responses to social change
> and its accompanying disorders. Both wanted to restore
> harmony to the social order, but Alessandri placed more
> emphasis on ameliorative reforms and the Right still pre-
> ferred coercion to concessions (Drake 1978, 470).

The POS presented its own presidential candidate in
1920, Luis Emilio Recabarren. Recabarren managed to cap-
ture 5 percent of the vote, but it was Alessandri who profited
from the decade of urban unrest, in spite of, or even because
of, the low voter turnout (only 4.5% of the population
voted). "Fear of the masses not the masses themselves elected Alessandri to the presidency" (Drake 1978, 53).

The increasing urban strife of the twenties lit a fire
beneath Alessandri's moderate reform platform. Besides
labor strikes against rising prices and falling wages, neighborhood organizers protested the exorbitant rents and poor
sanitary conditions of the tenements. The conservative elites,
however, "[had] decided to grant Alessandri a symbolic
victory only to quiet the lower classes. . . . [They] had no
intention of allowing the new president to become a dynam-
ic reformer, even within the limits of what reform meant to
Alessandri" (Drake 1978 54). The right-wing parties used
their control of the Senate to prevent Alessandri from passing a single item of reform legislation. They even rejected a
bill providing cost-of-living raises to the military. After
almost five years of political stalemate and growing urban
turmoil, the military, under the direction of Colonel Carlos

Ibañez del Campo, stormed Congress on September 5, 1924. "The military junta that succeeded Alessandri enacted a series of decrees aimed at removing oligarchical powers. . . . However, a group of young officers, viewing the performance of the junta as too weak, reinstated Alessandri as president on 23 January 1925" (Pollack and Rosencranz 1980, 7).

Alessandri then passed the 1925 Constitution, formally ending oligarchical power and establishing a strong executive. In 1927, however, the military again deposed the president and Ibañez appointed himself president of Chile (Pollack and Rosencranz, 1980, 7).

Ibañez defused protest by implementing the social programs proposed by Alessandri. Simultaneously, he ruthlessly attacked opposition political parties and independent labor organizations. Ibañez, for instance, extended and enacted social security and labor legislation. He also engaged in a major modernization campaign, building roads and schools, creating a central bank and Treasury, and implementing massive public works programs.

By this time, the POS had entered the Communist International (January 2, 1922) and already had become the Partido Comunista de Chile (PCCH). Although the Communist Party initially retained the personnel, goals, and structure of the POS, its growing ties to Moscow were to have important implications for the future. By 1925, its alliance with Moscow caused it to sever ties with other Chilean parties. By 1927, Moscow's influence led the PCCH to adopt a hierarchical and authoritarian political structure. It was Moscow's influence that encouraged the PCCH to support the dictator Ibañez over the reformist Alessandri. Inside the PCCH, these changes were bitterly debated. Recabarren, himself, was severely sanctioned, and he committed suicide a few years later. By 1929, the communist-linked Workers' FOCH had lost over 50 percent of its members. Many abandoned the labor movement, while others joined Ibañez's pro-government labor central (Bergquist 1986, 70; Drake 1978).

The Great Depression, the Socialist Party, and the Popular Front

In 1929, the Great Depression struck Chile. Work in the northern mining provinces grew scarce, dropping employment levels from 104,000 to 42,000 and forcing thousands of hungry miners and peasants to wander the country in search of work. Many miners moved to Santiago under the promise of alternate employment. Others simply drifted to the capital in search of work, settling in any way they could "under planks of wood and pieces of cardboard in the midst of garbage and despair" (Allende 1986, 134). Still others moved into the crowded tenement housing of their distant relatives, straining the city's fragile infrastructure and increasing the burden on Santiago residents, who also were struggling to survive. As the homeless population grew,

> [t]he dominant groups abandoned the central city areas in favor of selected portions of the urban periphery chosen because of their inaccessibility and favorable aesthetic and climatic conditions. Middle-level groups followed, moving in this direction as far as their means would allow. In Santiago the northeast was selected for this movement. Virtually all the upper and upper-middle urban sectors live in the northeastern barrio alto, extending from the

center of the city to the foot of the Andes. The rest of the urban periphery fell prey to the housing needs of the new lower classes, which also occupied decaying housing in the central city" (Portes 1971, 120–121).

Many new arrivals fell prey to speculators, and con men, who sold migrants titles to land that already had been sold (*loteos brujos*). Such widespread practices encouraged various tenants' alliances to form the Frente Nacional de la Vivienda (National Housing Front), in 1925 (Alvarado, Cheetham, and Rojas 1973, 46).

By 1927, growing poverty increased resentment against the second Ibañez coup, inciting university students to mobilize against the dictatorship. At the University of Chile's medical college, a student named Salvador Allende led the protests. The student movement acted as a catalyst, sparking a broad-based movement against the dictatorship. In October 1931, Juan Esteban Montero toppled Ibañez in a palace coup. Eight months later, Marmaduque Grove, a young Socialist colonel, overthrew Esteban Montero and proclaimed Chile a socialist republic. Twelve days later, Marmaduque Grove was himself overthrown. The short-lived socialist republic, however, left an indelible impression on the Chilean working class. For the next four months, instability within the military continued. Unable to quell its internal dissension, the military returned to its barracks in October 1932. Alessandri was reelected president, and Chile entered a long period of uninterrupted democratic stability.

The struggles of the twenties gave birth to a new Marxist party, the Partido Socialista de Chile (PS, Socialist Party of Chile), in 1933. The PS, founded by a radical middle-class intelligentsia, drew support from a broader, more diverse strata than had the Communists. In contrast with the Communist Party, which had emerged from the labor movement, the Socialist Party was born of an accord between intellectuals and professionals. The new party included nationalists opposed to the Comintern, Trotskyites opposed to Stalin, supporters of the 1932 twelve-day socialist republic of Marmaduque Grove, and students who had been active in the 1927 mobilization against Ibañez. Unlike the Communists, who preferred workers in the mining and manufacturing sectors—the "proletarian vanguard"—the Socialists "advocated a flexible and pluralistic policy" toward labor. They organized white- and blue-collar workers equally. This flexibility allowed the PS to survive the depression that wiped out many traditional Communist-linked mining and manufacturing unions. In less than four years time, the PS "had established itself as a leading political force with an electoral base that included manual and white-collar workers as well as students and intellectuals" (Faundez 1988, 29).

What the party lacked, however, was a strong collective identity. Indeed, Socialist success within the labor movement was "largely attributable to the enormous popular appeal of its leaders rather than to patient work by its militants at the grassroots level" (Faundez 1988, 29). In the 1932 election, for instance, the enormously popular Socialist leader Marmaduque Grove won 18 percent of the vote. This was three times the combined vote of the other Socialist candidates in Congress. While the Communist Party was tightly organized, disciplined, and class-based, the Socialist Party was a loose federation of cliques, factions, and *caudillos* (charismatic leaders, literally, leaders). This is similar to the difference between Communist and Social Democratic parties in Sweden observed by Adam Przeworski. The latter were forced to sacrifice the development of a strong class identity in order to appeal to voters across class lines. Both parties claimed to represent the working class:

> This was truer of the Communists, whose constituency and leadership were predominantly of that sector. The Communists were also the more organizationally solid of the two. The Socialists were a loose knit, electorally oriented alliance of left-wing notables. Communist party members and supporters were integrated into party structures at neighborhood levels. They were deeply involved in the party's work, familiar with its positions, and responsive to its leadership (Fleet 1985, 32).

Angelo Panebianco's work on party organization provides yet another explanation of the difference between the two parties. He argues that parties may organize by territorial penetration, territorial aggregation, or a combination of the two. Territorial penetration is a style of party organization in which the party begins at the national level and creates local and intermediary party associations. This style characterized the Chilean Communists after 1922. Territorial aggregation occurs when "local elites construct party organizations that are only later integrated into a national organization . . . [and are characterized by] decentralized and semi-autonomous structures, and consequently to a dominant coalition divided by constant struggle for party control" (Goldfrank 1993, 26; see also Panebianco 1988, 50). The Chilean Socialists epitomized this style.

Throughout the thirties, the relationship between the Communist and Socialist parties was one of bitter rivalry. Although both Marxist parties advocated collective ownership of the means of production, they fought over questions of agency, strategy, and tactics. The dispute was especially severe during the early thirties, when the Communists eschewed political alliances and attacked Socialists from the left. When the Communist Party attempted to form a popular antifascist front coalition in 1935, it was the Socialists who resisted incorporation.

The rivalry between the two Marxist parties opened new opportunities for the small Partido Radical (PR, Radical Party) which, until the World War I, had represented small capitalists in mining, agriculture, and manufacturing. In the twenties, the Radical Party began to draw support from white-collar workers in the expanded public and private sector and to make some inroads among industrial workers. In the late twenties, the party could count on the vote of 30 percent of the registered electorate. The creation of the Socialist Party in 1932, however, dropped Radical Party support to 18 percent. To win back the support of both blue-collar and the increasingly militant white-collar workers, the Radical Party rejected "the individualistic principles of liberalism and called for collective ownership of the means of production." It also "approved a resolution declaring that capitalism inevitably breeds class struggle and pledged to support the dispossessed classes" (Faundez 1988, 39).

Ultimately, the Radical Party's future was assured when the Communist Party persuaded it to join a Popular Front coalition along with Democrats and Socialists. The Radicals joined with the proviso that the Front back a Radical president. The Socialists had wanted to run Marmaduque Grove, but after the Communists insisted on the political expediency of a nominee from the Radical Party, the

Socialists reluctantly endorsed the candidacy of Pedro Aguirre Cerda. Soon after the establishment of the Popular Front in 1936, the Communist FOCh and Socialist-dominated unions consolidated under a single rubric, the Confederación de Trabajadores de Chile (CTch).

From 1938 to 1952, the Radical Party became the linchpin of Chilean democracy. It regularly formed electoral coalitions with the left-wing parties and betrayed their left-wing allies when they won election (Cavarozzi 1992, 212). Economic elites accepted a democratic system in which they were unable to win the presidency, in part because of their strength in a gerrymandered Congress, and in part because of the severe divisions between the two Marxist parties. This division allowed the Radicals to play the role of political broker.

In 1938, Pedro Aguirre Cerda was elected president of Chile. Several prominent Socialists assumed cabinet posts, including the Socialist physician Salvador Allende Gossens, who was named Minister of Health. The Communists refused to accept cabinet posts, hoping to dispel rumors that they intended to use the Popular Front as a means of seizing power. Instead they used their insider status in the coalition and outsider status in the government to organize within the labor movement. The strategy was enormously successful, and by 1940, they had displaced the Socialists in command of the CTch. The Communists' growing strength in the labor movement antagonized the Socialists. On December 15, 1940, Socialist leader Oscar Shnake "delivered a blistering attack on the PCch and presented the [Popular] Front with an ultimatum—either the PCch was excluded from the coalition or the PS would withdraw" (*La Hora*, December 16, 1940, cited by Barnard 1970, 351). On January 6, 1941, the executive committee of the Popular Front declared that the Socialist demand was unacceptable, and the Socialists withdrew from the coalition.

In 1941, Pedro Aguirre Cerda retired, after completing only half of his term. His death several months later added the final blow to the Popular Front. With the Popular Front on the verge of collapse, the right wing of the Radical Party reasserted itself, proclaiming the candidacy of Juan Antonio Ríos. The Conservative and Liberal parties joined forces now behind General Ibañez. The Marxist parties had no choice but to endorse Ríos, who won the 1942 election. Ríos appointed the Socialists to cabinet posts in the new administration, yet it was the Communist Party which profited from Radical rule.

> Through its alliance with the Radical Party the PCCh moved from the margin into the mainstream of Chilean political life. . . . By the mid-1940s, the PCCh had extended its activities into every social class and geographic region in Chile, it had created a formidable organizational machine capable of imposing an unusual degree of discipline on the membership, and it had displaced the Socialists as the dominant force in the country's largest trade union confederation, the Confederación de Trabajadores de Chile (Barnard 1970, 348).

The Great Depression and the import-substitution policies adopted by the Popular Front encouraged the migration of a quarter of Chile's population to Santiago. Many new migrants were members of Communist unions in the northern mining territories. These new waves of migrants helped the PCCh extend its base among the growing ranks of urban poor. "The irresistible impact of massive waves of migration overwhelmed the channels of integration of the traditional city and forced the emergence of a new plurality of interests and cultural orientations" (Portes 1971, 700).

Between 1940 and 1952 the size of the city grew from 10,985 hectacres to 15,047 hectacres. The southern district of Santiago experienced the greatest growth, while the wealthy began to move away from the center city and seclude themselves in the sparsely populated northeast (Centro de Estudios del Desarrollo, [CED] 1990, 15–58). At first *callampas* (neighborhoods that gradually sprang from shacks built illegally at the edges of popular neighborhoods, literally, fungi) grew along the periphery. The supply of land, however, "was limited, and, increasingly, staking out a home site in the outskirts of Santiago meant invading privately owned lands" (Schild, 1989, 63). The poor began to band together (usually with Communist support) to occupy property illegally, as in La Legua in 1946. From then on, callampas, were distinguished from *campamentos* (communities formed as the result of land seizures; Leeds and Leeds 1976, 223).

The arrival of urban immigrants to the city created a network of familial relationships and contacts that facilitated further urban migration. "Factory workers interspersed among nonindustrial poor in many neighborhoods; since many of the former were unionized and much of the union movement was Marxist influenced, the factory workers provided a core of established supporters in many urban neighborhoods" (Nelson 1979, 61).

By 1947, over 90 percent of Chile's working classes lived in these squalid overcrowded settlements. Communist Party organizing efforts often, thus, combined the issues of housing and work. Between 1943 and 1944, labor, under Communist and Socialist leadership, struck an average of

109 times a year, mobilizing over 43,000 workers each year. In 1945 and 1946, militancy increased even more dramatically and, labor struck a yearly average of 187 times, mobilizing 96,000 workers each year. "The growing militancy of workers intensified the rivalry between the Communist and Socialist parties, putting considerable pressure on the Radicals as each tried to win them over to its side," notes Faundez (1988, 70). By January, there was open warfare in the labor movement. "The PS denounced the PCCh for having made Chile into a battleground between the Great Powers, declared that the United States would soon be fighting Communism as it had fought Nazism, and told the PR that it would have to choose between cooperation with the PS or the PCCh—it could no longer have both" (*La Opinion*, January 17, 1946, cited by Barnard 1970, 358).

Toward the end of 1945, Ríos fell terminally ill and Vice-President Alfredo Duhalde Vásquez replaced him. Duhalde immediately turned on the Communist Party. With the support of the Socialist ministers, he arrested over one hundred Communist activists, including the director of the Communist Party newspaper, *El Siglo* (*El Siglo*, April 15, 1946, cited by Barnard 1970, 359). The harassment did not deter the Communists, however, from seeking a new alliance with the Radicals in the 1946 presidential campaign. This time, the Communists backed the candidacy of González Videla, a more left-leaning candidate within the Radical Party. When González Videla succeeded in winning the Radical Party's nomination, the Socialist Party presented its own candidate in opposition. Pablo Neruda and Julietta Campusano, two well-known Communist leaders, managed Gonzalez Videla's campaign.

González Videla won by a small plurality of 40 percent, against the Conservative Eduardo Cruz-Coke's 30 percent, the Liberal Party's 20 percent, and the Socialist candidate's 2.5 percent. Without a clear majority, González Videla was forced to make a pact with the Liberal Party, and Liberals assumed three cabinet posts. González Videla's government was also the first to include Communist ministers. This increased the legitimacy of the PCCh, and practically doubled its popular support, which previously had hovered around 10 percent. Within two months of González Videla's inauguration, the Communists had organized 358 new peasant unions with a combined membership of 11,000. By the end of the year, notes Faundez, "their popular support was almost twice that of the combined Socialist vote" (1988, 73). By the time congressional by-elections were held in 1947, the PCCh had increased its percentage of the electorate by 97.7 percent, capturing close to 18 percent of the vote (Gómez 1988, 365–366). The Radical Party, in comparison, had only increased its percentage of the vote by 53.07 percent (Gómez 1988, 101).

By the end of 1946, the Communist Party's impressive growth among labor and the urban poor was threatening to both Chile's economic elite and the United States. The Liberal Party refused to participate in the new cabinet unless the Communists were all expelled. Simultaneously, President Truman suspended U.S. aid and credit and launched an informal credit embargo in the World Bank and International Monetary Fund. The United States refused to lift sanctions while the Chilean Communist Party continued to function legally. Its international credit squeeze added fuel to a deepening economic crisis. Workers took to the streets in protest, and strike activity increased dramatically. González Videla responded to the growing turmoil by escalating his assault on both the Communist Party and labor in general. First, he suspended the registration of new rural unions. In April 1947, he accused the Communists of subversion and expelled them from the cabinet. By August 1947, he had ousted the Communists from their posts in the state bureaucracy.

Only then did the United States agree to support Chile's application for World Bank credit, approving an Exim-Bank credit for $23 million. The new loans, however, failed to placate the Communist-influenced unions, which continued to strike and march in the streets in defiance. González Videla turned to more draconian measures. In 1948, he approved the Defense of Democracy Act,

> a legislative enactment which banned the Communist Party, but which was also a fundamental attack on union rights and freedoms. The act gave the government power to cancel the electoral registration of nearly 26,000 members of the Communist party, to send the party's leaders into exile and to exercise direct political control over the composition and activities of the unions (Faundez 1988, 75).

Thousands of Communists were imprisoned, sentenced to concentration camps in northern Chile, or forced to flee the country.

The Poblador Movement and the Popular Unity

The repression launched by González Videla had a profound impact on the Communist Party. First, it deepened the Party's commitment to peaceful social change. When

Luis Reinoso, the organizational secretary, formed an army of *activos*, to battle González Videla directly, the rest of the Central Committee severely sanctioned him. Secretary General Galo González vehemently argued against the need for military action: "the realization of profound changes, of revolutionary forms is not necessarily followed in every circumstance by political action involving civil war, armed insurrection and violent, and extreme change. In our country there are examples that encourage us to think of the possibility of transforming the actual regime by peaceful means, i.e., parliamentary action" (Furci 1984, 56). Reinoso and the activos were evicted from the party (they formed a small splinter called the Bandera Roja, which never gained much support in Chile).

Second, it forced the party to abandon its traditional union stronghold, which had become the main target of repression. It moved to the poblaciones, where it gave priority to leagues of renters, neighborhood councils, and fathers' centers (Gómez 1988, 89). The repression convinced party organizers that they could not maintain support among the poor only by winning economic concessions at the workplace. Instead the party emphasized the development of an alternate political culture—linking the collective identity and world view of the poor to that of the party itself. Loyalty to the party was to be based, as Reinoso phrased it, on "people's faith in their own power, in the path of their own organization, in their own creativity as the only way to achieve satisfaction to all their aspirations" (Reinoso 1946, 15–19).

The repressive reign of González Videla also helped the pcch reach an accord with its old rival, the Socialist Party. Although González Videla attempted to extend the rivalry by offering the Socialists the cabinet post that had belonged to the Communists, he succeeded only in pitting the Socialists against each other. A small minority faction, led by Bernardo Ibañez, accepted the cabinet posts in the name of the Socialist Party, but the vast majority of rank-and-file members resisted. Under the banner of the Partido Socialista Popular (PSP, Popular Socialist Party), they banded with the Communists, creating an array of popular grassroots organizations. Under joint Communist/ Socialist leadership, Committees for the Homeless, Committees for Just Rents, Committees for Neighborhood Improvement, and Committees for Neighborhood Health Care flourished in the poblaciones. These myriad organizations became the basis of the Frente de Liberación Nacional (FLN National Liberation Front). "Unity at the grassroots and mass struggle became the central elements of Communist Party politics" (Gómez 1988, 88).

When the PSP decided to back Carlos Ibañez in the 1952 presidential election, the Socialist Party again divided. This time a small group led by Salvador Allende left the PSP and rejoined the smaller (PS), taking over its leadership. The PS now entered into a formal alliance with the Communists. In 1952, then, Chile had two Socialist parties: "the former [PSP], accounting for the bulk of the Socialist vote, had taken the populist option offered by the candidacy of Ibañez, the dictator of the 1920s: While the latter [PS], a party without significant following, had taken the first step toward the establishment of what was soon to become a durable alliance between the two Marxist parties" (Faundez 1988, 81).

The PS and PCch backed Allende in his first presidential bid in 1952. Ibañez was backed by an amalgam of factions from the traditional parties. The core of his support, however, was the Partido de Agricultura Laboral (PAL, Agrarian Labor Party), a corporatist-populist party ideologically located somewhere between European fascism and Argentine Peronism and sympathetic toward them both. Yet, although Ibañez won the 1952 election with 46 percent of the vote, the corporate-populist option was not successful in Chile. By 1953 the PS and PCCh had united the labor movement behind the newly formed Central Única de Trabajadores (CUT, Central Union of Workers). Housing issues also became critical as rural urban migration outpaced employment opportunities in the cities.

By 1953 economic difficulties had compounded the woes of the Ibañez administration. Inflation, which had averaged 12 percent in the first three years of his presidency, leapt to 56 percent. By 1954 it had reached 71 percent, and in 1955 hit a high of 84 percent. "This inflationary process, brought about by the collapse of copper prices after the Korean War, had a serious impact on the income of the wage earning population, increasing the militancy of the trade union movement" (Faundez 1988, 104).

Migration from the countryside and mining regions to the major urban centers, in particular the capital city, swelled dramatically. By 1952, over 60 percent of Chile's population was living in urban areas (up from 46.5% in 1920, and 52.3% in 1940). This led to an increase in the population of Santiago from .5 million (13.7%) in 1920 to 2 million (28.0%) in 1960 (Klaarhamer 1989, 177). The migration exceeded industrial growth, rendering the city impotent in the face of the growing demand for housing and forcing over 45 percent of Santiago's population to seek shelter in substandard or unsanitary housing (School of Architecture, University of Chile, 1952, cited in Urrutia 1972, 61). Before the end of the decade, the number of homeless in Santiago reached about 150,000 people, or 8 percent of the population (Schild 1989, 63; V. Espinosa 1988, 3).

To respond to the increasing pressures from the homeless Ibañez created the Corporación de Vivienda (CORVI, Housing Corporation)

> to continue the work of the Caja de Habitación [the government housing agency] . . . and in addition develop the first national housing plan, which included delivery of finished houses for middle-income groups. It also contemplated elimination of poblaciones callampas through delivery of plots to be followed by self-built homes for low-income groups. In addition the program contemplated an important housing subsidy to help low-income families cover mortgage payments. Ultimately, however, these subsidies, based on peoples capacity to save, benefitted high- but not low-income groups (Schild 1989, 63).

Ibañez's inability to provide a solution for the rapidly growing homeless population sparked a wildfire spread of committees for the homeless throughout greater Santiago. By the end of the fifties, the poblaciones had become a political battleground, with each committee of the homeless linked to a particular political party, all pressuring the government to provide a solution for the homeless. Residents of poblaciones learned to manipulate these political rivalries to their own advantage. As a result, Chile's poor developed an unusually high level of political sophistication.

Settlers soon learned that "they could not achieve anything without organization" (Lawner, 1987). By 1957, the Communist committees were both planning and organizing the illegal land seizures. They called meetings in the over-crowded tenements of the center city, drawing those "living with relatives in a [single] room; those dispossessed from center-city rooms scheduled for demolition for urban improvements; squatters on marginal lands; and renters of costly, cramped, inadequate quarters" (Goldrich 1970, 193). Juan Araya, president of the Communist Committee for the Homeless explains:

> From these committees, we created commandos to find land that would be appropriate for housing construction. When we found land, we spoke with the owners about its sale. Then we requested that the . . . Caja de la Habitación (Corhabit) buy the land and distribute it to those who applied. What usually happened, however, was that the government gave the land to people other than those who had originally applied. Thus, we decided to organize illegal seizures (Urrutia 1972, 73).

Communist and Socialist representatives then pushed for legislation to force the Caja de Habitación Popular (Popular Housing Fund formed by Alessandri in 1936) to buy the land for the settlers. The settlers, in turn, would buy out the government in rent. Within a set number of years the settlers would own the deeds to their homes.

It was the inability of the government to provide housing solutions for the poor that provoked the 1957 *toma* (illegal land seizure) of La Victoria. In 1956 several thousand people were living in misery along the banks of a river in San Miguel, an area called Zanjón de la Aguada. The following year a series of fires destroyed many makeshift huts along the river. Frustrated by the government's unwillingness to provide a solution, a group of residents began

CATHY LISA SCHNEIDER

The October 1986 anniversary celebration of the 1957 illegal occupation of La Victoria.

meeting to find their own. The most likely one to emerge was the illegal occupation of land. One original participant remembers that

> most of us were *allegados* [homeless, living in the homes of other people]. There was no government program to provide for the homeless. We began organizing for the land occupation six months early. We met clandestinely in different houses for an illegal land seizure.

Two days before the planned occupation, a fire left another two hundred people homeless, and increased the urgency for combined action. On October 30, 1957, three thousand families, organized by the Communist Party's Committee of the Homeless, occupied La Victoria in the first politically directed land seizure. The toma of La Victoria was a battle for immediate necessities as well as a battle for social and political change. "Through it settlers learned the power of solidary collective action" (Lawner, 1987). The police lay the seized land under siege, preventing food and water from reaching the illegal settlers. As one woman remembers:

> The police surrounded us. There were fifteen deaths from cold and disease. We faced fear by organizing. The solidarity was incredible. . . . We just stayed on the land until the government agreed to sell us the rights [to it].

For two months the battle between the pobladores and the police continued. Settlers organized teams for defense, to provide food, and for emergency health care.

Grassroots organizing in La Victoria did not end with the achievement of housing rights, however. "When we gained rights to the land we began to organize again," argues María, a representative to the Neighborhood Council from 1960 to 1964. They set up a governing body for the población called the Comando Poblacional, and held monthly assemblies in the street so all the residents could participate. They then set up block committees and allowed each block to elect two delegates to represent them on the Comando (Goldfrank 1993, 78). María explains:

> We formed the "Comando de Población" with committees on every block. We held elections with secret ballots and the Communist Party won. The first president of the community was a Communist, and he remained president until 1968 when he died. We always held elections by block, and the Communists always won.

Later they organized to seek help from the municipality, and from CORVI, for water, street lights, and the like. "There was no running water here," explains another of the original settlers:

> We petitioned Congress, and the Senate, there was little justice. We continued organizing efforts. Some students from the University of Santiago, then called Universidad Técnica, helped us. Only after three years of struggle and organization did we win water rights in 1963. Later we began to organize and fight for a health-care clinic. Then we created a school, of adobe with fourteen classrooms, and then a medical clinic. We had to organize to get a drug store, and a doctor. We got an NGO [nongovernmental organization, private foundation] in Germany to donate an ambulance. Everything we have, we won through struggle.

In the next few decades illegal land seizures would account for over 40 percent of Santiago's growth. Each seizure cemented the relationship between Chile's poor and Chile's political parties. By mid-century "Chilean politics was characterized by the development of strong political ideologically defined subcultures, whose shared assumptions of each ideology so deeply penetrated each subculture that they were passed through the normal process of socialization" (Constable and Valenzuela 1991, 141). "Chilean workers were more . . . inclined to view the world in terms of class antagonisms" (R. Kaufman 1976, 41), and Chile was "one of the most heavily ideological countries in Latin America" (Landsberger 1968, 219).

In 1956 the PCCh and the newly reunited Socialist Party united to form the Frente de Acción Popular (FRAP, Popular

Action Front, or FRAP). By 1958 the FRAP could count on a clear plurality among the urban poor. In the 1958 presidential election, for instance, 37.3 percent of those in Barrancas, 35.6 percent in La Granja, 36.8 percent in Conchali, and 40.6 percent of those in San Miguel voted for the FRAP compared to only 18.3 and 12.3 percent in the upper-class districts of Las Condes and Providencia, respectively (Nelson 1979, 351). By 1957

> most of the political groups which had supported Ibañez returned to their parties on the right and the left. . . . From then on Ibañez began to rely on the right-wing parties for political support, the government's economic policy became more coherent but bore no resemblance to its original national populist image (Faundez 1988, 105).

Much of the fallout, however, went to the Falange, a small party that had built support among the lower-middle class during the forties. The Falange, a forerunner of the Christian Democrats, was formed by religious Conservative Party youth attracted to the writings of the French Catholic philosopher Jacques Maritain. It rejected both the liberal principles of individualism and competition and the socialist principles of class conflict and state ownership of the means of production. Instead, the Falange advocated a return to basic Christian principles of charity and humility, "reconciling the need for economic growth with that for real social justice" (Faundez 1988, 134). Eduardo Frei, a leading ideologue of the Falange, helped translate abstract principles of Christian humanism into a concrete political program which called for, among other things, "more effective control over the country's natural resources and . . . the modernization of agriculture" (Faundez 1988, 134).

In a three-way split, Salvador Allende, the FRAP's candidate, lost his second presidential bid by a 1 percent mar-
gin, capturing 28.5 percent of the popular vote, to Jorge
Alessandri's 29.5. The newly elected conservative President Alessandri attempted to make inroads among the urban poor through government supported housing
construction and large scale urbanization. Simultaneously,
he called for the evacuation of hundreds of tenements in the
center city. Somewhere between 5 and 10 percent of Santiago's population were relocated during Alessandri's regime,
from callampas and *conventillos* (tenements) to massive low-
income housing settlements in the Southern district of La
Granja such as San Gregorio, José María Caro, Lo Valledor
and Joao Goulart (Schild 1989, 63; V. Espinosa n.d., 11).
The program, however, "failed to resolve the acute housing
shortage, exacerbated existing problems of inadequate infrastructure and social services, and furthered the spatial
segregation of wealth" (Schild 1989, 71; Valdes 1982, 98–99).
Furthermore, the high cost of the program clashed with the
regimes more conservative monetary policies. Alessandri
finally abandoned it in midstream, and in so doing sparked
yet another wave of illegal land occupations (Goldrich 1970,
193). By 1961,

> political forces re-aligned along well-defined ideological
> lines. Contrary to what had happened in the late 1940s
> when it had been possible to form broad coalitions which
> included governments made up of right-wing and Marxist
> parties . . . the right and left of the political spectrum had
> become irreconcilable extremes with the center parties
> gravitating around them (Faundez 1988, 128).

In the 1961 congressional elections the FRAP with "30

percent of the vote, became the largest electoral bloc in the country" (Faundez, 1988, 128). To head off the FRAP offensive, the right-wing parties forged a Democratic Front, but by 1963 the Democratic Front had exhausted its electoral pull. Leading members of the Chilean elite began to consider a military coup to prevent the 1964 presidential elections from taking place. American CIA operatives, however, calmed the conspirators by assuring them that the Christian Democratic candidate, Eduardo Frei, would win the 1964 election (Faundez 1988, 129).

The Christian Democratic Party (DC, Partido Demócrata Cristianos, sometimes referred to as PDC), an outgrowth of the Falange and sectors of the Ibañista movement, garnered only 15 percent in the 1961 congressional elections. By 1964, it controlled the largest voting bloc in Chilean history. Its phenomenal growth was in large part a consequence of a 1949 law giving women the vote. The increase in female voters tripled the size of the Chilean electorate, from 907,351 in 1952 to 2,917,121 in 1964 (Fleet 1985, 43), and the Christian Democrats won strong support among the new voters. The left-wing parties had difficulty appealing to women because of their historical link to the industrial proletariat, while the right-wing parties had little to offer any but the most wealthy. The Christian Democrats had the advantage of close links to the Catholic church, the one social organization with predominantly female members. In the 1964 election 62.9 percent of those who voted for Frei were women, and 75 percent were voting for the first time (Fleet 1985, 70).

The rapid increase in eligible voters also increased competition for support of the urban poor, who learned to manipulate the parties to their own advantage. Frightened by the growing poblador movement and the increasing strength of the Communist and Socialist parties, the Conservative and Liberal parties threw their support to the Christian Democrat Eduardo Frei. The u.s. government also supported Frei and contributed $2.6 million to his campaign, more than half his total expenditures. The strategy was successful. Allende, in his third presidential bid, won 39 percent of the vote, but Eduardo Frei, with both the center and right behind him, won the election with 55 percent. This marked the third time since 1938 that a president had won by a clear majority.

The political breadth of the DC support coalition gave the party an easy electoral victory, but, simultaneously, made governing extremely difficult. As Fleet notes, "the PDC was anything but a united or coherent political force as it prepared to assume power" (Fleet 1985, 78). The DC was torn by conflict within its ranks in each successive policy arena. Frei's capacity to reduce these conflicts depended on his ability to maintain high rates of economic growth and to improve the economic standard of living for the poor, without demanding sacrifice of the rich. His plans, however, rested on several erroneous assumptions. First, Chile's dependence on high interest foreign loans proved extremely costly and conflicted with the financial demands of the promised social programs.

Second, the government's "Chileanization" rather than "nationalization" of American copper mines meant that the Chilean government paid such a high price for its 51 percent share that the deal was an economic loss, particularly after the United States used its continued control of world copper prices to subsidize the Vietnam war effort.

Third, capital-intensive foreign investment increased

rather than reduced unemployment levels, as labor-intensive domestic-based industries crumbled under the threat of foreign competition.

Fourth, the land reform, intended to modernize agriculture, provoked bitter struggles in the countryside. The more radical Christian Democrats argued that the wording of the land-reform bill allowed landowners to use an endless array of court procedures and bureaucratic red tape to avoid losing their land. The bill allowed landowners to reserve the most fertile land (up to eighty hectares) and sell the rest to the government at inflated prices. Land given to peasants was often stripped of fertilizer and machinery. Landowners used their profits from the sale of this land to upgrade their machinery. Such technical improvements rendered agricultural labor redundant and swelled unemployment in the countryside.

Fifth and last, growing unemployment in agriculture increased migration to the capital, further straining the city's scarce resources.

The government's housing program, depended on both government and private funding. Those who applied for housing through the government's *Operación Sitio* (Operation Housing Site), received a plot of land, bought by the government from a private developer. Residents who built homes on this land or wished to repair homes in deteriorated condition could apply for government help through a program called *Plan de Ahorro Popular* (Popular Savings Plan), which supplemented an individual's savings account in private loan institutions. While many middle-income families could afford the savings plan, most poor families had to settle for a piece of land on the periphery of Santiago, and build their own 36 square meter home with wooden boards and nails. "The isolation of these settlements from the city intensified the spatial segregation of the poor" (Schild, 1989, 73–74). Sara Gajardo, Las Parcelas, Villa O'Higgens, and Lo Hermida were all established under Operación Sitio. As Leo recalls his early days in Las Parcelas, a población located on a mountain top overshadowing Lo Hermida in eastern Santiago:

> Las Parcelas was created under the system of self-construction established by Frei. Everyone constructed their own house, so there are some houses here five times larger than others. It depended on how much money you had. There were no organizations here. To get water we had to walk down the mountain. We had to steal electricity by throwing a cable over the electric wires. This was a very poor población.

Although almost 20 percent of Santiago's population (100,000 families) found housing of some sort through this program (Schild, 1989, 74; Valdes 1982, 99), within two years the government had run out of funds, and interest groups such as the Chilean Chamber of Private Builders and the savings and loan institutions had begun to use the program, almost exclusively, "as a means of producing profitable housing for middle-class families" (Castells 1983, 203). The second plank of the Christian Democratic program *promoción popular* (so named because of its goal of promoting popular participation), was more successful. Through it the government gave legal recognition and technical assistance to the *centros de madres* (mothers' centers), the *juntas de vecinos* (popularly elected neighborhood councils), *organizaciones deportivas* (sports clubs), and *organizaciones juveniles* (youth clubs). Over 21,917 organizations, with over 660,000 participants were created during these years (Oxhorn 1991, 76). In 1968 law number 16880 recognized the juntas de vecinos as "an expression of peoples solidarity and organization in the territorial realm whose aims were the permanent defense of members' collaboration with the authorities of the state and municipal governments" (Oxhorn 1991, 76).

Such attempts to expand political participation among the urban poor increased political mobilization at the same time as the government was slashing city services (Castells 1983, 203). The left-wing parties took advantage of popular discontent to increase their own electoral advantage in the poblaciones. They created alternative popular organizations, competing for control of those recognized by promoción popular, and finally leading new illegal land seizures. As Leo remembers:

> We had no choice, we had to organize. It was only through organization that we got the bus to climb the mountain to our village. It was only through organization that we forced the government to pave the roads. Many residents who had been active in left-wing parties at the workplace began to gather and create political parties here. . . . The Christian Democrats had a strong presence here, but they were passive. It was the left that organized for running water, sewage systems, transportation and construction brigades.

By 1969, "the Christian Democrats had lost control of the poblador movement and the neighborhood councils had become a political battlefield" (Castells 1983, 282). Between 1963 and 1967, it was La Granja, in the south, and Conchali, in the north, that had been the prime targets for land invasions. In 1967, for instance, the Communists occupied a section of the población La Pincoya and christened it Pablo Neruda, in honor of the famous Communist poet. The same year the población Villa Francia, in Estación Central was occupied by the MIR. By 1968, the left had turned their attention to the sparsely populated western zone of Santiago, Barrancas (now called Cerro Navia). Poblaciones such as Herminda de la Victoria, and Violeta Parra were seized under the direction of the Communist Party's Committee for the Homeless. One original settler of Herminda recalls:

> I had just arrived from the North, just in time to participate in the land seizure. At first I didn't want to participate. I said NO—things are too difficult—I don't want to live here. We didn't have anything!

Violeta, another settler recalls:

> I was eight-months pregnant at the time, and we were surrounded by police. A young infant died because we couldn't bring her to the hospital. The police threw stones at us. They refused to give us water. It was very painful. Entire families had to live in tents for months on end. It was because of this experience that we helped other settlers seize Violeta Parra. We knew what it was to experience hunger and cold.

It wasn't until the infamous confrontation, in March 1969, at Pampa Irogoín in Puerto Montt in which eight squatters were killed and seventy wounded by police gunfire that Frei abandoned the use of force in his dealings with the illegal squatters. The result was an unprecedented surge in illegal land occupations. The number of illegal land seizures increased from six in 1967, to twenty-seven in 1968, to

148 in 1969. Sectors three and four of Lo Hermida in the eastern zone were seized by the MIR, as were La Nueva Habana and several sectors of Villa O'Higgens, in the southeast district of La Florida. In the northern sectors of Remodelación, the Communists formed 20 de Mayo and Angela Davis. The growth in illegal land seizures was paralleled by a rise in strike activity from 1,100 strikes, mobilizing 300,000 workers in 1968 to 1,800 strikes involving 656,000 in 1970 (Faundez 1988, 152). Even illegal occupations of buildings and factories increased.

By the end of the 1960s even Christian Democrats were organizing illegal land seizures to compete with the left-wing parties for support among the urban poor. This created the unusual situation in which the poblaciones were both "a branch and a client of the political parties" (Leeds and Leeds 1976, 224).

> The poblador movement was created by the political parties. . . . 1. Each settlement depended on the political leadership which had founded it. Political pluralism was rare in the settlements, except between socialists and communists; and 2. The participation of the settlements in the political process was narrowly linked to the political line dominant in each community . . . we must speak of a branch of pobladores in every party rather that a "movement of pobladores" (Castells 1983, 282).

Not only were the settlements closely tied to the political leadership of the party that had founded them, but the character, culture, and identity of each neighborhood was shaped by this relationship. The right-wing Nationalist Party built a small base in the poblaciones through government housing programs and appeals to religion and tradition. These settlements were conservative, religious, and passive.

Settlements organized by the MIR were radical and explosive. Community leaders of these settlements were more often university students than pobladores. Although the MIR tried to involve población residents in the creation of minisocialist states, the needs of the población remained subordinate to those of the party. Their social role

> shifted according to the political tasks and priorities established by the MIR at the national level. In the first year, MIR supported urban demands as a means of consolidating its position in the squatter movement so as to reinforce its militant power. . . . [When] MIR announced that top priority should be given to the penetration of the organized working class . . . cadres were sent to other political duties (Castells 1983, 206–207).

The MIR's lack of roots in such poblaciones was partly a result of both its *foquista tendencies*, or emphasis on a military strategy in which it played vanguard, and its tendency, like that of the other more radical left-wing parties during this period, to ride the crest of popular mobilization (E. Kaufman 1988, 160). *Poder Popular* (Popular Power) was seen as a phenomenon whose development was distinct from the organization and development of the party itself. The party operated as vanguard in such communities, providing the organization and military force to challenge the reformist, albeit socialist, state; but it did not integrate the pobladores into the ranks of the party. As Leo recalls of the MIR toma in Lo Hermida:

The MIR organized the settlement along military lines, as if they were already living under socialism. They actually convinced part of the population that this was socialism. They tried to control all aspects of poblador life, even aspects of family life. Residents really resisted this . . . the majority of MIR leaders weren't even from the población.

Similarly, Gabriel Salazar, an ex-member of the MIR recalls:

Originally most tomas were led by the Socialists and Communists, but, as they began to put the breaks on the mobilization, the MIR would take over and force a rupture with the rest of the Left. From the beginning the MIR supported more autonomous settlements with vigilance committees to fight crime, popular health clinics with visiting doctors, and popular courts, thereby creating small solidary autonomous societies.

In one infamous case of popular justice, the committee castrated an accused rapist, opening up a national debate over popular justice. As time went on, notes Salazar:

The MIR became more and more focused on creating a military defense system. They began to recruit pobladores for military defense teams and to pay less attention to the creation of minisocialist states. As the MIR put more emphasis on military strategy, the pobladores were relegated to second place. Such experiences weakened and disillusioned residents of MIR settlements. The MIR began to throw pobladores out of the party for failing to respect military leaders. I defended the pobladores and was also thrown out of the party.

"The . . . existence of a deep gap between the vanguard of MIR militants, who pursued a revolutionary political line, and the other residents [continued]. For the latter, involvement in the political struggle was a matter of access to land, houses, and services." For the MIR militants, however, the campamento was "above anything else, an organizational weapon of a revolutionary party" (Klaarhamer 1989, 181).

Settlements controlled by the Christian Democrats, by way of contrast, were individualistic, and lacked strong grassroots networks. They were dependent on state resources, and even those formed by illegal land occupations abandoned political activity once their housing needs were satisfied. In them, as in the southern Italian communities described by Robert Putnam, the "patron client relations involve[d] interpersonal exchange and reciprocal obligations but the exchange [was] vertical and the obligations asymmetric. Furthermore, the vertical bonds of clientalism seem[ed] to undermine the horizontal group organization and solidarity, of patrons and clients alike" (Putnam 1993, 175).

Even after new organizations arose, these poblaciones remained divided by income, status, and political affiliation. As Leo recalls:

> It was always difficult to organize in Las Parcelas. There was so much differentiation. Some houses were quite nice, others were little more than shacks. Some worked in construction, but more were self-employed, many as gardeners or servants of the wealthy in Las Condes. When we did organize, we confronted much resentment.

Even when the Christian Democrats led their own

illegal land settlements "the campamento [was] a tactical vehicle for the short run, its power to be later eroded or rendered rhetorical rather than real" (Leeds and Leeds, 1976, 225). The leaders of Christian Democratic poblaciones "set themselves the task of negotiating with the authorities which they perceived as suppliers of goods and services" (Klaarhamer 1989, 180). The church was often the only institution in such poblaciones to encourage organizing at the local level. As one poblador recalls:

> The Hogar de Cristo [House of Christ], in particular, was very important. They worked with left-wing activists to help residents construct their homes.

Lastly, settlements organized by either the Communist Party or the FRAP were tightly organized, semiautonomous, and led by skilled grassroots leaders. Socialists usually participated in such settlements through the Comando de Pobladores sin Casa (Committee of the Homeless), which was originally organized by the FRAP, but dominated by the Communists. These communities tended to have a higher percentage of organized workers than other poblaciones (Castells 1983; Goldrich 1970, 185; and Portes 1969 and 1976), and their residents displayed a strong "sense of solidarity . . . and tendency to perceive that some degree of interdependence promoted the resolution of [their] problems" (Goldrich 1970, 191–192).

In a 1969 survey of four poblaciones, Alejandro Portes observed, residents of Herminda de la Victoria, the Communist dominated población, were more likely to belong to a union, and to display a high level of political efficacy. They demonstrated a high level of class consciousness, social cohesion, and class solidarity. For example, 60 percent of the respondents showed great confidence in their locally elected leaders. Only 21 percent of those in the Christian Democratic housing project, 38 percent of those in the Christian Democratic land-grant community, and 47 percent of those in the callampa felt the same. Fifty-four percent of respondents in Herminda felt that their neighborhood councils could help them a great deal, while only 18 percent of those in the housing project, 26 percent of those in the land-grant community, and 44 percent of those in the shantytown felt the same level of confidence in their locally elected leaders. Thirty-eight percent of those in the housing project, and 16 percent of those in the land-grant community felt that their neighborhood council couldn't help them at all, but only 3 percent of those in Herminda displayed such lack of confidence in their local political leadership (Portes 1969, 37a).

When asked if they believed that they could change a government decision that adversely affected them, the vast majority of pobladores in every población answered yes (81% land occupation, 81% shantytown, 93% land grant, 56% housing project). The lowest sense of efficacy was found in the housing project, where the government had supplied the community with everything (Portes 1969, 39a).

Portes also discovered, in all of the poblaciones, but especially in Herminda de La Victoria, the Communist led población, a "strong and clear class identification, that considering the specific obstacles and difficult situation of these groups, had remained latent, but could easily, given the right set of circumstances, flower and affect future courses of action" (Portes 1969, 39). When asked if the rich were rich because they had sacrificed or because they had exploited the poor, for instance, 81 percent of respondents in

Herminda compared to an average of 57 percent of respondents in the other poblaciones believed that most of the rich attained their positions by exploiting the poor (Portes 1969, 34). Twenty-four percent of respondents in Herminda saw their poverty as a consequence of either the class structure (20%) or the objective situation in the country (4%). Only 12 percent of the respondents in the other poblaciones felt the class structure was the principle reason they had not attained the situation to which they aspired. The poorest población, the shantytown Parque Santa Monica, showed the lowest percentage rating class structure as the cause for their poverty (7%) and the highest percentage blaming their poverty on personal failure (37%) (Portes 1969, 34). Thus despite the extreme suffering and deprivation in the poorest shantytowns, rebellion was weak. The poorest of the poor blamed themselves for their poverty.

But Portes's original survey did not distinguish between the organizational experience of the land occupation and the socializing influence of the Communist Party. It was impossible to make this distinction in the first survey, since Herminda was an illegal land occupation community, but one organized by the Communist Party. In a later work, Portes addresses this question directly.

In a study of four communities, two of which were exposed to Communist Party influences, and that had at the time of the study Communist neighborhood councils—one a squatter settlement and one a government project—and two of which were not exposed to communist influence—again one a squatter settlement and one a government project—Portes discovered "respondents in Communist-influenced areas were distinct in their support of radical measures" and that this radicalism "increased with greater time of residence in the area," regardless of whether the Communist-dominated community was originally an illegal land occupation (Portes 1976, 107). (See table 1.) "While the experience of a land invasion is itself a socializing experience," he observes, "since land invasions give participants

TABLE I

Political Radicalism in Lower-Class Settlements of Santiago, 1968–1969

	INTENSIVE COMMUNIST PARTY INFLUENCE	CHRISTIAN DEMOCRATIC INFLUENCE
Percent supporting the elimination of private property	48	20
Percent believing the revolution was good for Cuba	55	33
Percent believing that a revolution would be good for Chile	44	26
Percent believing that authentic social change should only include the poor and go against the rich	39	27
Percentage believing that authentic social change can only be attained through revolution	34	22
Percent endorsing the use of force as the only means to attain authentic changes	39	28
Percent supporting Communist and Socialist parties	64	24

SOURCE: Alejandro Portes and John Walton, *Urban Latin America*, (Austin, 1976): University of Texas Press, reprinted with permission.

a sense of their own collective strength and bring them into direct confrontation with the police, press, legislators, and government officials . . . these visceral experiences need not have been translated into a socialist consciousness." In other countries the "purposeful intervention and socialization by political agents" led the squatters to interpret their experiences in a variety of different forms (Portes 1976, 103). In Chile, however,

> Communist socialization attempted to present the invasion and subsequent confrontations with government and landowners as practical lessons in the class struggle. The effective help provided by the Party on these occasions was aimed neither at purely electoral support nor at participation within the existing order but rather at *drastically changing the dominant ethic among these groups*. Its goal was to effect a transformation of basic needs into a clear understanding of the structural origins of poverty and the necessity of class solidarity (Portes 1976, 105; emphasis mine).

This purposeful socialization and direction provided by the Chilean Communist Party, Portes insists, accounted for the high levels of class identity and radical militancy in such communities.

In a later study, Daniel Goldrich stressed the critical role played by the Communist Party in the political development of the poblaciones. In a 1970 survey, Goldrich found that politicization (which he defined as an "individual's awareness and psychological involvement in politics, his image of himself as an active participant or passive agent in it, the accessibility to him of channels leading to political decision-making and his participation in politics") was lowest in the población that had experienced the most repression during the land occupation (the Peruvian población Espíritu). This seemd to imply that the land invasion experience was a depoliticizing one, especially if the invasion was illegal, and thus met with repression (Goldrich 1970, 186).

Yet, in Chile, squatters who had participated in illegal land occupations were more politicized than those who had not. The explanation of this paradox was that the relationship established between the invaders and the Chilean Communist and Socialist parties, before, during, and after, the invasion, increased the squatters internalization of collectivist norms. "While severe negative sanctions depoliticize, *external support at a time of a great stress contributes to the capacity to withstand that stress without subsequent depoliticization*" (Goldrich 1970 192; emphasis mine).

Still, those pobladores that had participated in the land invasion and received support from the political parties did not always internalize radical collective norms. Those associated with the Christian Democratic Party tended to cease political activity soon after they resolved their immediate housing needs.

> Only the FRAP seemed to effect the transition in the politicization of the activist from the immediate, pressing housing need to a focus on more fundamental problems. . . . The Chilean data provide evidence that the activist poor who support the FRAP tend to maintain a sense of solidarity and make the transition, in their thinking about politics, from the acute to the equally acute, but less vulnerable, set of economic needs. . . . . *The significance of the* FRAP *organization and the invasion experience as a politicizing agent is indicated by differentially high local*

involvement of FRAP *invader groups as opposed to 1.* FRAP
*noninvaders and 2. Christian Democrats and nonaffiliated
invaders who either do not develop or do not sustain high
politicization* (Goldrich 1970, 192, 185; emphasis mine).

The FRAP and the Communist Party, in particular, imbued participants with a collective identity, a sense of their
own efficacy, and a strong political commitment. Residents
of these communities displayed higher degrees of politicization, political efficacy, and solidarity, and they were more
likely to transfer the collective experience of the land occupation to other arenas of political activity. Fifty-nine percent of the residents affiliated with the FRAP, for instance,
compared to 20 percent affiliated with the Christian Democrats conceived of taking economic or educational problems
before officials.

> There is a direct relationship between politicization and
> disposition to work collectively. . . . As the poblador
> becomes more aware of and involved in politics, he comes
> to perceive that some degree of interdependence pro-
> motes the resolution of his problems. . . . Though both
> parties at the leadership level promote ideologies valuing
> organization and collective action of the poor, only the
> FRAP seems to effect the internalization of this principle in
> its poblador adherents (Goldrich 1970, 191).

These social and political differences were often reflected in the physical layout of the poblaciones. The Christian Democratic poblaciones tended to be the most
differentiated, with wooden houses provided by Operación
Sitio located next to brick or concrete buildings of various
sizes built by private owners next to tin shacks, tentatively
assembled by the poorest members of the neighborhood.

Roads were often no more than flattened dirt. While some houses had backyards and chicken coops, barely any houses had grass or greenery, and even trees were sparsely planted.

The Mirista poblaciones tended to be the poorest since they were the most recently constructed and were built with few resources. Though many of the Mirista campamentos were eradicated during the dictatorship, those that survived continued to look like campamentos, with flimsy wooden houses, dirt floors and roadways, and wooden outhouses in the backyard.

The appearance of the Communist poblaciones depended on their age. Their distinguishing feature, however, was the similarity of the homes. As Carlos Albrecht, an architect called in to give advice on many new poblaciones, recalls. "I had in mind more spacious living quarters with parks and grass, but the settlers were adamant. They wanted the población designed like a fort with narrow passage ways and no open spaces. Each house was to be constructed identically." In older Communist poblaciones, such as La Victoria, houses were built of concrete, each one immediately next to the other. In new poblaciones, such as Herminda de la Victoria, the houses are still made of wood plank and are about ten by forty meters in size. Most have wood floors as well, but the wind and rain whistle through the houses in the winter. In Yungay, the newest, residents live in small brick apartments in buildings constructed by the dictatorship. The more well-off residents paint their inside walls, but the others leave the brick raw. The apartments are less than half the size of those built under Frei, and offer no protection against Chile's frequent earthquakes. I will return to these distinctions in chapter four.

By the end of Frei's term, massive social spending had led to soaring inflation. Frei was forced to cut most of his social programs, but the massive mobilization of the urban and rural poor continued unabated. The mounting demands on the government split the Christian Democratic Party in three.

The *rebeldes* were the most radical. They favored extended reforms and structural change. In 1969 they abandoned the DC and created Movimiento de Acción Popular Unitaria (MAPU United Popular Action Movement), which became, together with the FRAP parties, the basis of the Unidad Popular (Popular Unity coalition) in 1970.

The *terceristas* were more conservative than the rebeldes, but also supported an extension of agrarian reform, the nationalization of foreign enterprises, and workers' self-management in the factories as the first stage of the building of a communitarian society. Their success in nominating their candidate, Radmiro Tomic, to compete with Allende in the 1970 election cost the Christian Democrats the support of the traditional right, including the remaining right-wing third of their own party.

This right wing of the Christian Democratic Party had supported the modernization and anticommunist aspects of the DC program but had opposed its more redistributive and communitarian policies. They particularly disliked the land reform, the workers' self-management program, and the government's increased spending on housing and urban services. When Tomic was nominated to succeed Frei, most of these Christian Democrats gave their votes to the right-wing candidate Alessandri. In the three-way presidential race, Tomic had the lowest showing of the three candidates: 28 percent, to Allende's Popular Unity with 37 percent and Alessandri's National Party with 35 percent.

Allende's election in 1970 was a consequence of the

intense political mobilization and polarization that had begun under Eduardo Frei. It was also a catalyst, intensifying the "revolution from below," and with it the reaction from the right (Winn 1986).

In many ways, Allende's program was no more radical than that of Radmiro Tomic. Like Tomic, Allende called for the nationalization of copper and large monopolistic sectors of the economy. For Allende, however, the nationalizations would represent the first stage in a slow democratic move toward Socialism. The bulk of Allende's policies were Keynesian, rather than Marxist. In the first year he concentrated on raising minimum wages and expanding social services to the poor. He nationalized the copper companies with unanimous approval in both houses of Congress. He nationalized banks legally through the stock exchange, later using them to finance massive social programs. Increased demand stimulated production, and the workers' share of national income rose by 10 percent. By the April 1971 municipal elections, the Unidad Popular had increased its mandate from 37 percent, in the 1970 presidential election, to 51 percent.

The left's gain at the polls had two dramatic consequences. First, it convinced grassroots political activists that they had the mandate to move ahead with their proposed transition to socialism. Second, it convinced the right that a concerted effort would be needed to block the proposed transition. The Nixon government, international lending agencies, and domestic and international businesses launched a campaign to "make the economy scream" (CIA director Helms, in U.S. Senate Select Committee on Intelligence 1975, 227). The closing of international credit and the shortage of foreign exchange, coupled with skyrocketing demand as a direct result of both wage increases and expensive social programs, led to massive shortages and spiraling inflation.

A political crisis exacerbated the economic crisis. Until 1973 political pact making, coalition building, and compromise had been the linchpin of Chilean democracy. The system had begun to disintegrate in the sixties because of the Christian Democrats' uncompromising rule. Now, however, it was dealt a final, mortal blow as 1. the political right circumvented the democratic state through direct sabotage and subterfuge; 2. the political center boycotted the process of congressional negotiation and; 3. the political left used constitutional loopholes to bypass Congress (Garreton 1986, 115).

The inability of the state to mediate the growing conflict increased political competition at the grassroots. Between 1970 and 1973, the number of illegal urban land seizures rose tenfold and accounted for one-quarter of the growth in the shantytown population of Santiago (from 300,000 in 1970 to 400,000 in 1973). Most of these land seizures were led by the MIR and the more left-wing Socialists, but even the Christian Democrats led a few, mobilizing opposition from the right.

The Communists, during this period, stood staunchly behind the government, using their political power to create model housing settlements (such as Villa Lenin, renamed Yungay after the coup) and pushing for official recognition of autonomous political structures such as *juntas de abastecimientos y precios* (JAP, neighborhood organizations used to ration and distribute scarce necessities), *cordones industriales* (self-managed factory councils), and *tribunales vecinales* (peoples's courts) "based on existing experiences of grassroots justice" (Castells 1983, 201). Unlike the MIR, which saw the creation of Poder Popular as a means of pushing the government toward socialism, the Communists viewed these organizations as fortifying government support against both left- and right-wing opposition. Although Congress blocked legislation recognizing the legality of these new forms of popular organization, grassroots activists maintained such organizations in a voluntary, quasi-legal form.

By 1973 the crisis had reached a climax. Workers and peasants engaged almost daily in illegal factory and land seizures, while opponents of the Unidad Popular attempted to block their activity through terrorism and sabotage. Leo recalls:

> During this period even the Communist Party illegally seized land, but we seized it to help the government, to make sure that reforms were not reversed. We were willing to pay for the land. The MIR wanted everything free, because the government was socialist. The Christian Democrats occupied land to destabilize the government.

Despite the severity of the crisis, Allende's support among the poor held firm, and in the 1973 congressional elections the Unidad Popular won 43 percent of the vote (less than its vote in the municipal election but 6% more than it had won in the presidential election).

The Christian Democratic Party, now controlled by its most right-wing faction and representing a middle class plagued by shortages and rapidly escalating prices, allied with the right-wing Nationalist Party. Together they won 55 percent of the new congressional seats. The elections failed to give the Unidad Popular the majority it needed to overcome the congressional boycott, and the opposition coalition failed to win the two-thirds it needed to impeach Allende.

On June 11, 1973, a group of military officers attempted to overthrow the government, but the more constitutionalist officers thwarted their effort. The following day the number of illegal factory and land occupations doubled. Radicalized workers seized control of entire sections of the city (cordones industriales), expropriating industry, electing neighborhood councils, and forming peoples' courts. Pobladores, directed by the MIR, attempted to surround the upper-class neighborhood of Las Condes with radical, militant, lower-class encampments (often supported militarily by the MIR). Although Allende preempted most of these illegal settlements, opponents of the Unidad Popular, used such activities to play on upper- and middle-class fears. They argued that the squatters would eventually control all of Santiago. Soon wealthier neighborhoods were creating committees for neighborhood defense. By mid-1973 the Christian Democrats were calling for military support against Marxist totalitarianism.

At a conference held in Lo Curro, the Unidad Popular debated whether to "consolidate by advancing" or "advance by consolidating" (Winn 1986, 234–235). The Socialists favored the former, arguing that the government must prepare for the worst. They supported arming the factories and seizing the commanding heights of the economy. The Communists insisted that the only way to avoid a military coup was to retreat, to consolidate gains, and to negotiate with the Christian Democratic Party. This would weaken the procoup element of the military and strengthen the hand of the constitutionalists. Allende sided with the PCCh. In

August he signed a series of agreements with the Christian Democrats, guaranteeing he would return illegally seized factories to their original owners and confiscate illegally stashed arms. The Christian Democrats, however, were suspicious. Instead they introduced a congressional *acuerdo* (agreement) with the support of the Nationalist Party, accusing the government of attempting to establish a totalitarian system in Chile. During the third week of August the measure passed, 81 to 47.

On September 7, two more carabinero generals joined the procoup conspirators. The remaining constitutionalist officers within the military were no longer able to deter insurrectional activity. On September 8, the Christian Democrats called for a national meeting. They suggested a measure by which both the president and the Congress would resign, and new elections would be held to resolve the crisis. On September 11, 1973 the armed forces occupied Santiago. Tens of thousands of political leaders, workers, students, and pobladores were arrested. Tanks bulldozed entire towns. Many poblaciones, such as La Legua, La Victoria, and Herminda de la Victoria, fought the armed forces, using nothing more than their own crudely made weapons for days on end. No town alone could resist the force of the Chilean military. Within weeks the military had destroyed all forms of popular organization. "The scope and intensity of the repression reflected the extent and depth of popular mobilization in Chile by September 1973. It was an ironic tribute to the success of the revolution from below" (Winn 1986, 248).

CHAPTER THREE

Repression and the Consolidation of Authoritarian Rule

At dawn, the navy gathered its troops in Valparaiso. By 10:00 A.M. army tanks had surrounded the presidential palace in Santiago. At 11:00 CARABINEROS (the police) began to assault the Moneda, and at promptly 1:00, the air force joined the attack, shelling the palace from the air. Leo, then a young poblador, living in Las Parcelas, remembers watching the Moneda burn from his home on the mountain. Several days later he found bodies in the river. "Every day after that more, often three or four," he recalls. "I began to hear stories. There were so many people who had simply disappeared."

Ana was working in Las Industrias, where they were bombarding the factories.

> Tanks and helicopters surrounded us. A friend told me they had killed my husband and that I must flee before they arrested me, as well. I was pregnant, and over fifteen miles from home.

Ruth, eleven years old on the day of the coup, remembers the terror:

> I was in class when they suddenly told us to go quickly, directly to our homes. I remember my rage, because when I arrived home—I had these rabbits, and my father had given me a cat as a gift and the cat had killed the rabbits and torn their eyes out. It was like a sign, blood everywhere, and these eyes covered with blood. . . . We knew they were killing people and we didn't know how many were dead. I remember hearing machine-gun fire day and night. I was only a little girl, but from that moment on I didn't feel like a little girl.

There was no pretence of legality at this stage. All four branches of the armed forces engaged in open repression. "Civilians opposed to Allende [eagerly reported] any information they had on their colleagues or their neighbors to the military" (Frühling 1984, 360). The violence appeared like the convulsion of society itself. "A revolutionary insurrection against the government had taken place, and those who had led it were not completely sure about their own forces, much less about those of their enemy. Consequently, the intensity of the repression was extremely high, and it was applied capriciously, since the armed forces did not know who their targets were" (Frühling 1984, 352). It was not simply the lack of information that accounted for the intensity and seemingly arbitrary nature of the repression. Unlike military regimes in Brazil, Uruguay, and Argentina, the Chilean military had deposed a government passionately supported by almost half the nation. It could not, therefore, simply eliminate its enemies in secret. Instead, it used brutal, calculated, and public terror to frighten the population into submission. In the poblaciones associated with the left-wing parties, the military arrested or shot at residents almost indiscriminately (Leeds and Leeds 1976, 243 n. 3). As Rosa, a Communist living in Herminda de la Victoria, recalls:

> The military surrounded the población. Day and night we heard shooting, and saw helicopters overhead with search lights. It was unbearable. We couldn't get out, we couldn't fight. Then people started to disappear. Some they killed right here. I remember them shooting a woman and her three children here on the street.

They scattered the bodies of the dead throughout the poblaciones, as both a symbol and a warning to potential opposition. As Violeta remembers:

> Every day new bodies arrived, nude and headless. They floated in the river. We were stunned. It wasn't possible. We cried, please no more. They took my husband on the twelfth. A police patrol arrived. My youngest son was only thirteen years old. The wife of my older son was six months pregnant. She was disappeared. Her son still goes to sleep under the bed. In this way we learned that anything was possible.

The military deployed search and destroy missions throughout La Bandera, La Legua, Roosevelt, La Pincoya, José María Caro, Remodelación, and Yungay, and the industrial centers Sumar, Aerolite, Elemental, and Mademsa (Commission on Truth and Reconciliation 1991, 25). Hernán recalls a typical scene in La Pincoya:

We saw a long line of men marching with their hands over their heads escorted by a military patrol. Then began the searches. They arrested both my brother and my father. They put all the men in the football field and began to select among them. Most of those they took never returned.

Yet, there were few cases of armed resistance in even the most combative poblaciones. As one journalist who lived in La Victoria during the coup, observes, "there were no armaments, no preparation or central leadership. Residents confronted tanks, alone."

Even the least political poblaciones suffered the regime's wrath. The military dismantled the networks of organization the pobladores had created, taking control of the neighborhood councils, arresting the popular leaders and replacing them with their own supporters. In Las Parcelas, Leo recalls, they arrested and tortured the president of the neighborhood council and dumped the disfigured bodies of two other members of the council on the street. They replaced them with military appointees, people with "a tremendous hatred for the people they were supposed to represent."

The military divided Santiago into four military zones. Each branch of the armed forces controlled a different zone. The air force occupied the southern zone, the red belt. Here, they held prisoners in makeshift jails. In Valparaiso, they confined them in ships. In Santiago, they crowded them in football stadiums. In the other regions they filled concentration camps such as Pisagua in the North or Dawson Island in the South, with prisoners.

They tortured indiscriminately. Routine methods included the use of violent blows, which produced fractures and hemorrhages. Prisoners were forced to lie on the ground with their mouths pressed to the floor, without moving, for days on end. They stripped the prisoners and held them under constant light or, alternatively, deprived them of light by bandaging their eyes, so that they lost all sense of time. Many were kept in solitary confinement, in cubicles so tiny that it was impossible to move. They deprived all of food, water, clothing, and sanitary facilities.

Some prisoners were hung by their wrists for extended periods, or submerged in foul-smelling liquids or excrement. The soldiers almost always raped the female prisoners. Sometimes they raped and tortured them in front of family members or with animals (Commission of Truth and Reconciliation 1991, 24).

The regime's victims fell into nine categories:

1. Popular members of the deposed government, in particular those involved in social programs or popularly elected.

2. Labor organizers, grassroots leaders, such as those belonging to the neighborhood councils, mothers' centers, or JAP's.

3. Mapuche Indians who had been involved in the land reform programs.

4. Students, usually university students.

5. Members of left-wing political parties whose political affiliations were deduced from their participation in conflictual activities such as strikes, land occupations, or protest actions. These prisoners often were identified by landowners, industry owners, or neighbors.

6. Government sympathizers without any known political affiliation. Most of these were poor and had participated in actions designated as "conflictive."

7. Victims of political vendettas.

8. Victims of personal vendettas.

9. Those seized for a range of offenses from delinquency, alcoholism, or drug abuse to violations of curfew (Commission on Truth and Reconciliation 1991, 25).

There was "no screening process which permitted the government to distinguish the political relevance of those jailed. . . . Some were brought to courts of martial law, others executed without trial" (Frühling 1984, 353). One example of the capricious nature of repression during this phase was the execution of sixty political prisoners in Calama. The prisoners, all of whom had been tried in military courts and sentenced for terms ranging from twenty days to sixty years, suddenly were seized from jail on December 19, 1973, and executed the same day (Frühling 1984, 353).

Sometimes victims were told that they were free and then were shot in the back. Other times, they tortured prisoners to death for no apparent reason other than to inflict suffering. The body of Eugenio Ruiz-Tagle, for example, showed signs of extreme abuse. He was missing an eye, had his nose and ears cut in two, displayed severe acid burns on his face and neck, had a broken neck bone, severely swollen lips, cigarette burns, and severe bruises. Victor Jara, the famous folk singer, was brutally beaten in front of thousands in the Chile Stadium. His hands and face were severely disfigured, and he was shot forty times.

In Santiago, they executed over five hundred prisoners in the last three months of 1973. In Valparaiso, political executions topped two hundred. Between one hundred and five hundred were murdered in Concepción and Antofagasta. Altogether 1,261 civilians were executed between September and December of 1973. Military officers were not immune. On the contrary, the military aimed the first martial law trials after the coup, against itself. "The regime had to devise mechanisms to purge officers who had been committed to the former government or who seemed dangerously disaffected" (Arriagada 1988, 141).

On December 27, 1973, the regime accused a group of air force officers of plotting to defend the Allende government (the notorious Plan Z). Prosecutors argued that "before the coup there had existed a de facto state of war in the country, which allowed the martial law court to investigate crimes committed before the state of war was formally declared" (Frühling 1984, 354). This allowed the government to declare all members of parties of the Unidad Popular to be enemies of the state and, therefore, "guilty of treason for providing the u.p. government and its parties— the enemies—with military secrets" (Frühling 1984, 354). The government's declaration of war granted military authorities extensive powers in dealing with left-wing activists and gave legal jurisdiction to courts of martial law. "The use of martial law as a means of repression, particularly the trial of political dissidents by courts of martial law, was the first explicit manifestation of the National Security Doctrine" (Frühling 1984, 353).

Article 4(c) of the Law of National Security prohibited assemblies designed "to propose the overthrow of the constituted government or conspire against its stability." Article 6(i) accused those who called, without government authorization, for "a public act in the streets, plazas and other places of public use," of endangering national security, and subjected them to military jurisdiction. Decree Law

77 prohibited participation in any of the parties that made up the Unidad Popular coalition of Salvador Allende and subjected violators to military tribunals.

Pinochet also suspended the Officers' Assessment and Appeals Board. From September 22 on, decisions about promotions and retirements were "exercised exclusively by the Commander-in-Chief of the Army" (Arriagada 1988, 142). Decree Law 220, issued on December 24, 1974, created a new body, the Officers' Extraordinary Assessment Board, which could be convened only by Pinochet himself. The new board gave Pinochet power not only to take "decisions on colonels' promotions and retirements away from the Assessment Board," but to put promotions to the rank of general under the "exclusive province of the Commander-in-Chief" (Arriagada 1988, 143). The Commander-in-Chief could also "waive the fulfillment of one or more requirements for promotion except that for time served in grade" (Arriagada 1988, 144).

Pinochet declared a state of siege, banning the left-wing political parties and suspending all others. He prohibited unions from holding elections, depriving union leaders of the workers' mandate and increasing the gap between the union leadership and its base. He required police authorization for all public meetings and assemblies. The military dismantled all the popular organizations in the poblaciones and changed the names of poblaciones themselves "with the intent of removing progressive cultural symbols" (Walker 1986, 48). Such policies were designed to provoke intense fear and helplessness, not only among left-wing activists, but among the poor and working class as a whole. The long-term objective was not only to "destroy the left as a political and ideological alternative" but to "restrict political and cultural thinking that could challenge the government" (Frühling 1984, 355).

Pinochet dismantled social services and returned nationalized industry to private owners. He also pursued policies designed to redistribute national income upwards, securing windfall profits for large sectors of the Chilean elite. The regime freed prices, reduced corporate taxes, and eliminated net wealth and capital gains taxes, levying, instead, a 20 percent value-added tax. Simultaneously, Pinochet devalued Chilean currency by 230 percent. These policies, when combined with the assault on labor, had devastating economic consequences (Ffrench Davis 1983, 909). In the first three months, inflation soared to 1,000 percent (Ffrench Davis 1983, 909), raising rents for the poor by tenfold, forcing entire families to abandon their homes. As houses were abandoned in middle- and upper-class neighborhoods, such as Providencia, Las Condes, and La Reina, housing deficits in the poorer neighborhoods, such as Penololen, La Granja, Cerro Navia, San Ramón, Pudahuel, La Pintana, La Florida, and El Bosque, billowed. While the former showed a dramatic increase in space per person, the latter showed an even greater decrease, evidence of extreme overcrowding (CED 1990, 15–28).

In 1974, the regime attempted to control inflation by contracting the rate of expansion of the money supply and by reducing real wages, which dropped by 30 percent (Cuadernos de Economía 1982, 84). The increase in costs more than tripled the increase in the quantity of money, and triggered a severe recession (Foxley 1983, 53). By 1974 wages averaged $.07 an hour (in constant u.s. dollars) compared with the $.38 an hour they averaged the year before the coup (Chossudovsky 1979, 68). The working-class share of national income dropped from 65 percent to 40 percent (Brown 1980, 272), and unemployment doubled in the first three months, to 7 percent, and then continued to rise, reaching 13.3 percent in the first quarter of July. By 1975 the average income of the poorest family was 46 percent of its 1973 level (Sherman 1991, 67; Volk 1983, 5–6).

These policies did not only affect the working class and the poor. Strong business groups, which for years had pressured successive governments for expensive subsidies and protection, now appeared impotent. The passivity of this sector was a direct consequence of their feeling "of having lived through a definite threat to their existence during the u.p. government" (Stepan 1985, 100). As the former president of the right-wing Nationalist Party put it:

> I don't regret anything, neither the absence of political parties, nor the absence of parliament for the last seven years, because I believe that the construction of a free society could only have been achieved without them. . . . We were at war, and what you do in wartime is defend yourself. . . . I simply believe that a government of authority is required for the entire period needed for Chile to be converted into a modern nation" (cited by Stepan 1985, 323).

One might even go so far as to argue that the Chilean state represents a step beyond Bonapartism. Instead of exchanging the right to rule for the right to make money in the classic Bonapartist transaction, significant fractions of the Chilean bourgeoisie abdicated the right to rule and the right to make money in the short run in the hopes of preserving class privilege in the long run (Stepan 1985, 321).

The Secret Repression: 1974–1976

After the brutality and violence of the coup, civilians lost their taste for bloodshed and grew reluctant to inform on their neighbors. The military needed a new method of continuing the war against what was now a clandestine enemy. On June 24, 1974, Pinochet created the Dirección Nacional de Inteligencia (DINA, Directorate of National Intelligence). The DINA was an elaborate, secret police network directed by Pinochet's personal friend Manuel Contreras, which functioned independently of the rest of the junta. The DINA centralized "the intelligence gathering process and . . . executed repressive policies in one specialized agency . . . [to] diminish the costs involved in the repressive process . . . and distinguish more clearly which targets were really dangerous" (Frühling 1984, 360).

The creation of the DINA marked the beginning of a new phase in the repression, characterized by secrecy and "disappearances." As the Commission of Truth and Reconciliation reports, the period between 1974 and 1977 "corresponded to a carefully devised and centrally coordinated plan to eliminate an entire category of people" (Commission on Truth and Reconciliation 1991, 101).

The Servicio de Inteligencia de Fuerza Aérea (SIFA, Air Force Intelligence Service) operated parallel to the DINA but was controlled by the air force. The air force later replaced the SIFA with the DIFA (Dirección de Inteligencia de la Fuerza Aérea), which eventually became the Comando Conjunto. The Comando Conjunto had the express purpose of eliminating the Communist Party in the southern zone of Santiago. Ana, of Yungay, recalls:

I was working with Adrián Saravia, the party's regional

secretary, trying to recreate popular organizations. First they arrested Saravia. Then Weibel, then Basoa. The case of Saravia hurt most. They said it was he who had turned informant, giving the names of the entire regional party. I had known him very well, and couldn't believe that he would betray us. I didn't know who to trust. Bernardo and I had to go into hiding since he knew us so well.

The intelligence agencies, of the police and navy, were smaller than either the DINA or the Comando Conjunto. The police agency, Servicio Inteligencia de Carabineros (SICAR, Police Intelligence Service) was subject to the command of the DINA. The navy agency, Servicio de Inteligencia Naval (SIN), acted mainly in Valparaiso and Concepción (Commission on Truth and Reconciliation 1991, 101).

Between 1974 and 1976 over six hundred party and organizational leaders "disappeared," almost all of them members of the underground left-wing parties. In 1974, the government focused its energies on eliminating the MIR, and most of those disappeared were militants of that party and "to a lesser extent militants of the Socialist and Communist Parties" (Frühling 1984, 361). The vast majority of disappeared, in these years, were young people, in particular university students (Commission on Truth and Reconciliation 1991, 108).

In 1975 they aimed the repression against the Communist Party, and by 1976 "almost all the people who disappeared were members of the Communist Party" (Frühling 1984, 361). Most of the disappeared Communists were older than those of the other parties. Many had been union organizers, popularly elected grassroots political leaders in the poblaciones, or members of the deposed government. Two consecutive central committees of the Communist Party and of the Communist Youth were eliminated in these years. The former security agent Andrés Valenzuela confessed to some particularly brutal examples of summary executions:

> We had about forty detained. . . . We hung them by their hands and feet and applied electric current. . . . One of them was about fifty. . . . We hung him in a shower and since they had applied electric current earlier he was very thirsty. He opened the tap with his mouth to drink, but a sentry arrived and turned it off. He turned it on again. Finally we let the water run. We let it run all night falling on his body. In the morning he was dead from bronchial pneumonia.
>
> It was 1975 when we were battling the Communist Youth. An air force helicopter arrived and took (from the secret torture center in Colina) between ten and fifteen of them. . . . They gave them drugs, but it appeared that the drugs failed to take effect because they were aware of what was happening. . . . One prisoner awoke during the flight and they had to "give him one." Later they started throwing them into the sea. . . . They said they had to open them first . . . cut open their stomachs so they wouldn't float (Andrés Valenzuela 1985).

For the DINA the main enemies were the MIR, the Socialists, and the Communists. For the SIFA, DIFA, and later Comando Conjunto, the MIR and Communist parties were more dangerous. Both intelligence agencies attempted to destroy the left-wing parties by physically eliminating their members. Individuals with political experience, education, and courage, as exemplified by their refusal to break under torture, were considered the most dangerous and irredeemable, and, therefore, they executed them first (Commission on Truth and Reconciliation 1991, 107). Many victims during this period were women. Nine of the women disappeared were pregnant (Commission on Truth and Reconciliation 1991, 107).

Prisoners were held in clandestine torture centers such as Tejas Verdes, Londres 38, José Domingo Cañas, the infamous Villa Grimaldi, or the Discoteque, also known as La Venda Sexy. In Londres 38, where they held prisoners during the last months of 1973 and throughout 1974, they preferred the *parrilla*, a metal mattress to which a prisoner was strapped, nude. Electricity was then applied to the prisoner's lips, genitals, open wounds, and, when available metal prostheses. Prisoners were often tortured in front of relatives or loved ones. At times, family members were kidnaped, tortured, or raped in front of the prisoners.

In José Domingo Cañas, used mainly between August and November of 1974, they held prisoners in a "hole," approximately one by two meters, without windows or ventilation. Sometimes they kept as many as ten prisoners in the same hole.

In Villa Grimaldi (used from the middle of 1974 through the summer of 1975) they separated prisoners into chambers known as the tower, the Chile house, and the Corvi house. The soldiers locked prisoners in small wooden closets in the Chile and Corvi houses, subjecting them to intense torture at random hours of day and night. During their stay prisoners were unable to wash, change their clothes, or use sanitary facilities. Food was of poor quality and insufficient quantity. The most common method of torture was the parrilla, but prisoners were also strapped to a metal *camarote*, which had two levels. A friend or family member of the prisoner would be placed above or below and tortured simultaneously (Commission on Truth and Reconciliation 1991, 105).

Another common procedure was to hang prisoners by their wrists or wrists and knees. The weight of their bodies over long periods would compound the agony of the electric shocks. They would submerge other prisoners in vats of excrement or filthy liquids, to the point of suffocation. Sometimes they would put a plastic bag over their heads (a "dry submarine") to induce asphyxia. Occasionally they poured boiling water on the prisoners as punishment. In other cases they ran over the prisoners' legs with a truck.

The last chamber, the tower, originally used to store water, was so small that the detained were forced to remain on their knees. Often two or more prisoners were forced to share this cramped space. Most of the prisoners in the tower arrived after extremely intense torture sessions and were never seen again.

In La Venda Sexy the military preferred sexual tortures such as rape. Other common tortures included the "telephone," in which the torturer boxed the prisoners ears until deafness set in, and the kidnaping of the prisoner's family members (in particular those not involved in politics), who they subsequently tortured or raped in front of the prisoner. Fourteen-year-old Sandra Caro, from La Legua, for example, was kidnaped, tortured, and raped to punish her father, a union leader. Soldiers raped María Pía de Silva, from Pudahuel, ten times in front of her ten year-old-son, and forced her to watch as they burnt her three-month-old daughter with cigarettes. Rape with animals was also common. Verónica DeNegri, for example, was raped repeatedly with rats.

The secrecy surrounding these centers allowed civilians to absolve themselves of direct responsibility for the repression.

> In 1976 especially, detention for political reasons occurred without witnesses. People detained were questioned in secret prisons and without witnesses. . . . Selective repression against the left encouraged people's passivity . . . since it considerably narrowed the number of targets, it helped to create a climate of normalcy in the daily life of the country (Frühling 1984, 361).

By the middle of 1974 the rivalry between the air force and the army had led to an intense competition between the air force's secret police, the Comando Conjunto, and the DINA. The rivalry between these two torture agencies accelerated the value attached to new information and multiplied the number of deaths from excessive use of force. In December of 1974 the air force executed three members of the Comando Conjunto who were suspected of giving information to the DINA. Andrés Valenzuela, a former member of the Comando Conjunto, gives a dramatic account:

> Bratti Cornejo was a colleague of mine, a soldier in the Air Force . . . we killed him in the Cajón del Maipo with the Communist informant Flores . . . because they [Bratti and Flores] tried to move into the DINA . . . the chiefs met and decided that it was treason because they would pass information to the DINA and as a result the DINA would arrive before us to execute an operation. . . . They accused him [Bratti] of treason because he worked with the DINA (Andrés Valenzuela 1985).

By 1975, DINA's power was virtually unlimited. It commanded an empire of thousands and counted on the active collaboration of both civil and state enterprises such as the national telephone company, the national railroad, the merchant marine, the national airline, the Ministry of Foreign Affairs, and foreign diplomats. It also maintained active relations with foreign governments such as the Argentine, Uruguayan, and Brazilian military juntas, with which it had an elaborate network of surveillance and repression called the CONDOR. The DINA also maintained informal ties with Cuban exiles living in the United States, as well as with Argentine and Italian terrorists, which facilitated its activities abroad, such as the assassination of Orlando Letelier in Washington and General Prats in Argentina and the attempted assassination of ex-chancellor Bernardo Leighton in Italy (Commission on Truth and Reconciliation 1991, 102).

The growth of DINA paralleled that of the army, the police, and the police detective service, the three branches of the armed forces controlled directly by Pinochet. While the budget for the armed forces as a whole nearly doubled between 1973 and 1980, the budget of the air force and navy dropped by 10 and 22 percent, respectively in 1976. In 1980 their budgets were only 32 and 38 percent higher than they had been in 1973. The budget for the army, on the other hand, rose steadily, increasing 10 percent in 1976, and 76 percent by 1980. The comparison is even more dramatic for the police and police detective service. Their budgets rose to 29 and 82.4 percent respectively in 1976, and 99 and 272 percent in 1980 (Varas 1984, 247).

Pinochet's gradual consolidation of personal power was reflected in the army's growing dominance in the cabinet as well. In 1973 each branch of the armed forces had three members in the cabinet, and the position of president of the Republic was to rotate among the junta members. By 1974 the army held five cabinet positions to the three held by members of the other military branches. The 1975 cabinet was two-thirds civilian: eleven civilians (many of them, including the minister of the economy, Christian Democrats) to five officers. The air force was left with only the Ministry of Labor.

The economic model advocated by these new civilian ministers (known as the Chicago boys due to their adherence to the monetarist economic model advocated by Milton Friedman and his colleagues at the University of Chicago) complemented the political by dwarfing "the socioeconomic role of the state, . . . transferring its functions to the private sphere, . . . [and] disarticulating previously organized interests that might challenge the Pinochet regime" (Borzutzky 1987, 27). Under the Chicago boys' influence, the Chilean economy was drastically altered. Social services, protective tariffs, subsidies, low-interest state loans, and price controls were abrogated; the state bureaucracy was liquidated or turned over to the private sector; and large sections of nationalized industry were auctioned off, far below their market value (by 1976 more than four hundred firms had been privatized). One or more of the five clans (extended families that own industry, agriculture, and finance) with access to foreign currency bought most of them. Most prominent among the new clans were Cruzat-Larraín and Javier Vial's "pirañas." These financially-based clans began to replace the more traditional ruling families in the hierarchy of wealth and power. The government repaid public sector debt through private sector borrowing, enriching the financial clans at public expense. It cut all other government expenditures, so total expenditures fell by 27 percent in real terms in 1975, while public investment was reduced by half (Foxley 1983, 56).

In 1976, Nicanor Díaz, the minister of labor and a close friend of General Leigh, proposed the establishment of government-run unions. The construction of such unions would strengthen the air force by giving it an independent base of power. Pinochet responded by replacing Nicanor Días with José Piñera, and naming another Chicago boy, Sergio Fernández, to head the Ministry of Interior. Piñera's labor legislation prohibited both government and industry-wide unions and restricted collective bargaining to the plant (Volk 1983, 9).

Interest rates were freed, justified as part of the process of economic liberalization and within six months had soared from a real rate of -23 percent in the second quarter of 1975 to 178.4 percent by the third quarter of the same year (Foxley 1983, 57). Coincident with the freeing of interest rates was the dramatic lowering of external tariffs (Foxley 1983, 57). Their removal, when coupled with the elimination of subsidies and low-interest state credits and low consumer demand, created serious difficulties for internal producers. By the middle of 1975, Chile was suffering an economic depression surpassed only by that following the 1929 crash. By 1977 agricultural production had fallen 27 percent while construction had dropped by more than 31 percent, throwing seventy-five thousand construction workers into the streets (employment in construction dropped from 175,000 in 1973 to 100,000 in 1978) (Brown 1980, 272).

The new economic model dealt its most staggering blow to the textile industry, which formerly had been a center of left-wing activity. The reduction in tariffs and subsidies encouraged a flood of low-priced imports, increasing textile imports from $25.7 million in September

1976 to $62.9 million in May 1977. Of the two thousand companies operating in 1974, four hundred had closed by 1977, while others remained heavily in debt or passed to other hands (*Latin American Economic Report* July 1977). The collapse of the textile industry had dramatic consequences for the urban poor. Over seventy-three thousand textile workers lost their jobs as employment in textiles dropped from one hundred twenty-three thousand in 1973 to fifty thousand by 1978.

The destruction of the construction and textile industries, Santiago's two largest, increased poverty levels in the capital city to 57 percent in 1976 (Ffrench Davis, Raczynski, and Raczynski 1990, 37). Incomes in San Miguel and La Granja dropped from approximately fifty thousand real pesos per capita to fifteen thousand and thirteen thousand respectively. Unemployment swelled as high as 80 percent (Universidad de Chile 1986; Angell 1991, 202). The struggle to survive, in such poblaciones, became an end, absorbing the pobladores' time and energy.

Mining, another traditionally militant left-wing industry, was also hit hard. Among non–copper miners sixth thousand lost their livelihood, with employment dropping from one hundred five thousand in 1973 to forty-five thousand in 1978 (*Latin American Economic Report* July 1979, 216).

The government's solution to the employment crisis was to create two minimum employment programs. One, the Programa de Empleo Mínimo (PEM, Minimal Employment Program), was begun in April of 1977. The second, Programa Ocupacional para Jefes de Hogar (POJH, Occupational Program for Heads of Households), was initiated five years later. By 1985 these programs employed 12.1 percent of the work force at 40 to 67 percent of the minimum wage

(Sherman 1991, 74; Oxhorn 1991, 74). Pobladores with a political history, or those who currently belonged to apolitical social organizations such as soup kitchens, were refused even this minimal assistance.

During the same period the government began to liquidate entire shantytowns, under the guise of market logic. Shantytown eradication, particularly in areas of high-value land, the government argued, was necessary to allow the real estate market more freedom. Operación Confraternidad (Operation Fellowship), initiated in 1976, for example, forcibly relocated hundreds of families to the furthest periphery of the city, generating "a wave of fear among the pobladores of poblaciones and campamentos," (Valdes 1987, 27) and exacerbating the divide between the rich neighborhoods and the poor.

Government aid to state agencies providing technical assistance was also severely cut during this period. The entire Corporación de Reforma Agraria (CORA, Agrarian Reform Agency) was eliminated after nineteen years of work, the reversal of the land-reform law having removed most of its functions. Public sector employment dropped from 18.3 percent in 1972 to 13.2 percent in 1977, according to official figures. By 1981 personnel in the various agricultural agencies (ODEPA, CORA, INDAP, SAG, CONAF, IDA) had been reduced by 80 percent from 26,282 in 1973 to 5,139 in 1980. In addition, the state sector's wage bill was cut, falling 20 percent between 1972 and 1977 (Departamento de Agricultura de Chile 1982, 37).

These measures, which entailed a dramatic increase in overall unemployment, would have been impossible without the dictatorship. The stringent measures in the economic sphere were paralleled in the political one, where

Pinochet and his junta made good on their promise of
order—not by keeping tanks in the street but by creating
the illusion that no valid opposition existed. . . . The
facade consists of laws that have been abundantly commented upon. . . . The facade is the normalcy of daily life
in the streets of Santiago. . . . The reality from the point of
view of this inquiry is the existence of another world—the
world of those arrested, detained in camps, tortured, disappeared, found dead or released without real possibility
of finding gainful employment (Americas' Watch, April
25, 1983, 7).

The lack of protest in 1975 then was not, as the military
insisted, because no valid opposition existed, but because
no organizations could survive. The left-wing parties were
in retreat, the popular organizations destroyed, labor unions
had been eliminated by the collapse of industry, and the
government was cohesive and strong. The 1974 economic
crisis did not stimulate protest activity, because unlike the
1981–1983 crisis, it did not weaken the government. "The
key point to understand about the shock plan is that, unlike
the equally severe recession of 1981–1983, the 1975–1976
recession was desired: it was the conscious policy of the
government" (Volk 1983, 6).

The Institutionalization of the Regime

An upsurge in inflation during the first quarter of 1976
encouraged the regime to overvalue the peso by 10 percent.
In March 1977 the regime again revalued the peso and
announced a thirty-day value for future exchange rates

(Foxley 1983, 57). It also deregulated external capital flows and slashed tariffs across the board to a maximum of 10 percent. These policies had several consequences. On the one hand, the revaluation of currency began to have some impact on inflation, and real wages began to recover. The Chilean economy also experienced considerable growth in nontraditional exports, such as fruits, seafood, and lumber. These export industries profited from low wage rates, favorable exchange rates, and tax exemptions granted all exported goods (this included exemptions from both across the board value-added tax on all products sold in Chile and from export customs duties) (Foxley 1983, 72). The 1964 agrarian reform enacted under Frei stimulated export agriculture under Pinochet. The large inefficient estates, which had previously characterized Chilean agriculture, were never returned to their original owners. Instead, Pinochet auctioned them to the highest bidder. Rising land prices fostered a capital market in land as owners of medium size holdings were encouraged to sell, and those with access to foreign capital were eager to buy. "The privatization of the reformed sector," observes one economist, "led to the elimination of the asentamientos [agrarian reform settlements] that formed the basis of the old unions" (Kay and Silva 1992, 228). As Gerardo Munck notes:

> The simple elimination of most peasant organizations was part of the changes in the Chilean countryside that led to the emergence of capital intensive agriculture, especially in the dynamic categories of production such as fruits, forestry, and certain leguminous plants. . . . Due to the capital intensive nature of the new agriculture, . . . fewer peasants owned land, as even those peasants who benefitted

> from privatization of the reformed sector surrendered to
> the high prices being offered for their land. . . . The nature
> of work changed as more permanent rural workers were
> replaced by temporary workers (Munck 1994, 197).

Export-led growth in agriculture dramatically altered the
ecological balance in the countryside leading, down the
line, to massive deforestation in the 1980s and causing the
extinction of six species of seafood. Simultaneously, it increased rather than decreased the unemployment crisis in
Santiago.

In Santiago the only growth industry was finance, as
low cost, negative real interest rate loans became widely
available. Local interest rates were high and international
rates were low; reloaning and speculation was encouraged.
The large family clans with holdings in banks, agriculture,
and industry transferred their investments into the more
lucrative financial and speculative markets. Although pro-
ductive investments dropped by 14.6 percent in 1979, and
manufacturing output dropped by 22 percent, the credit
boom opened new jobs in finance and services. By 1979
unemployment had dropped to 13 percent, down from 16
percent in 1978. Yet the percentage of Chileans living in
poverty continued to rise, from 28 percent in 1969 to 36
percent ten years later. Caloric intake for those Chileans in
the bottom 20 percent had dropped, in the same period, by
more than 7 percent.

The drop in manufacturing had its most profound impact on young people between the ages of fifteen and twenty-
five. They were, by now, the largest age group in the
poblaciones, because of declining birth rates. The industrial
proletariat, during this period, both shrank and aged. In

1971, 24.3 percent of blue-collar workers were between the age of fifteen and twenty-four, ten years later, this proportion had decreased to 9.5 percent. Young people were also disproportionately more likely to be without work. In 1970, 5.1 percent of the adults were unemployed as were 9.9 percent of the youth. Ten years later, 7.7 percent of the adults were unemployed along with 25.9 percent of the young people. By 1982, 18.1 percent of adults were unemployed, and 36.2 percent of young people. Furthermore, young pobladores were more than twice as likely to be unemployed as young people from other parts of the city (J. Weinstein 1991, 262–263).

High unemployment among young pobladores did not stimulate radical political action. On the contrary, young people, in 1980, were more likely to classify themselves as middle class and less likely to classify themselves as workers than older persons in similar situations (J. Weinstein 1991, 264). Instead of increasing political activity, the high rates of youth unemployment stimulated increased drug use and delinquency, particularly in the poblaciones. In 1970, according to one study, only 34 percent of the young people had smoked marijuana. There was no difference in the rates of young people of different social classes. In 1989, 34 percent of young people still admitted smoking marijuana. The percentage of smokers living in upper-class neighborhoods, however, had decreased to 8.2 percent. In middle-class communities it had decreased to 13 percent. It had increased to 54.1 percent in poblaciones (J. Weinstein 1991, 267). Furthermore, 64.1 percent of pobladores felt that there had been a marked increase in delinquency (J. Weinstein 1991, 269).

After 1979 Pinochet began to shift his method of

political control from direct repression to "a policy of containment of opposition" (Frühling 1984, 366). The selectivity of the repression was accentuated with the aim of consolidating the political and economic model. In August of 1977, largely due to pressure from the United States (a consequence of both President Carter's human rights policy and new revelations about the role played by the DINA in the Letelier bombing in Washington), Pinochet dissolved the DINA. He replaced it with the official sounding Central Nacional de Informaciones (CNI, National Center of Information). From 1978 onwards, Pinochet increasingly relied on the authoritarian rule of law. As Frühling notes, "a new legal framework emerged which was designed to include every act of power of the government within the limits of legal rule" (Frühling 1984, 367). With labor unions weak, the middle classes passive, and the economic elite firmly behind him, only General Leigh and the air force posed a threat to Pinochet's absolute power. In 1978 Pinochet discovered a mechanism to eliminate that threat and simultaneously quell international criticism, in particular that of the United Nation's Commission on Human Rights.

In January 1978 Pinochet held a National Consultation referendum; the text, imposed on other members of the junta, read, "I support General Pinochet." The referendum's intent was to strengthen Pinochet's personal authority within the military apparatus. It was an overwhelming success.

> The overwhelming, but questionable support obtained by General Pinochet was then used as a new source of legitimacy for the military government. It also transformed Pinochet into the undisputed leader. The plebiscite allowed General Pinochet to root his personal leadership in

the "will of the people," to eliminate the other members of the Junta, and to increase his control over the military (Borzutzky 1987, 28).

Six months later, on July 24, 1978, Pinochet accused General Leigh of plotting against him and conspiring to organize a new military coup. He evicted Leigh from the junta, and replaced him as commander of the air force. The entire Cuerpo de Generales (corp of generals) of the air force, nineteen air force generals, resigned in sympathy.

In 1978, Pinochet began to privatize the state itself, beginning with the social security system. "By fragmenting union collectivities, by passing large parts of the social security apparatus and public health into the private sector, and by imposing free choice anti-monopoly rules on unions and professional associations, the Pinochet state apparatus launched a long range attack on the organizational potential of the opposition in civil society" (Stepan 1985, 323). The typical loci of struggles over wages or housing, were fractured—each individual forced to confront a different enemy.

State cuts in housing, health care, and education dramatically effected the poor. The problem of housing became particularly urgent as the state cut housing expenditures by 35 percent. Between 1978 and 1980, one-third of the households formed in Chile were unable to find housing (Sherman, 1991, 73; Klaarhamer 1989, 185). By 1985 nine hundred twenty thousand people suffered from the housing shortage, while twenty thousand new housing units were unoccupied because their prices were too high (Sherman 1991, 75; Leiva and Petras 1986, 113).

In 1978, the government initiated yet another relocation program increasing housing density in the periphery and decreasing it in the four wealthiest neighborhoods (Las

Condes, La Reina, Providencia, Nunoa). Operación Confraternidad relocated 1,850 families from neighborhoods near the city center to the southern periphery of Santiago, more than a two-hour bus ride from downtown and their place of work. "After living in places with adequate or excellent services," notes Julia Paley, "the newcomers arrived at locations with the worst services in health, education and transportation" (Paley 1994, 87).

The eradications, notes Paley, "explicitly sought to homogenize the different areas of the city by social class" (Paley 1994, 85). Pedro Guzmán Alvarez, mayor of La Granja, for instance, explicitly referred to the class character of the surrounding community in explaining, in a letter to the housing authority, why the government should move a campamento in Las Condes to La Granja: "These lands, because of their location, cannot be used for the construction of basic housing [low-income housing] but rather a much higher level, in accordance with the population that exists in that area" (P. G. Alvarez 1982; Paley 1994, 85).

The thousands of new arrivals strained the social networks of the older poblaciones, undermining the resident's sense of trust and security. As one poblador interviewed by Paley, observed:

It was quite sad to arrive here. . . . People that had lived their entire lives here had dreamed of having a house like this one . . . had more right than we did. . . . I never wanted this house, and we took the possibility from them. For this reason we had more difficulty at the beginning. The people robbed us, . . . [my brothers] were assaulted, beaten up (Paley 1994, 89).

The eradications created "fractured and mistrustful

passageways. Divided from each other, people were unlikely to even leave their houses" (Paley 1994, 91).

In 1984, the government initiated a new round of eradications, forcing the relocation of yet another 25,977, and increasing the total number of eradicated families to 28,703 families by 1985. The number of people living in Santiago's slums and shantytowns grew to 1.3 million. The percentage of families living as allegados (with more than three persons per bedroom), grew from 25 percent in 1965 to 41 percent in 1985. A new type of living situation became common; 23 percent of families lived in some type of makeshift housing in the backyards of friends or relatives. By 1985 there were two hundred fifty thousand homes of this kind (J. Weinstein 1991, 252).

The shortage of housing especially affected young people. In a 1984 study of three poblaciones, Eduardo Valenzuela found that only 24 percent of young married couples had a home of their own. Fifty-four percent lived with their parents, and another 21.6 percent lived with families to whom they were not related. Furthermore, 57 percent of those between fifteen and nineteen, and 66 percent of those between twenty and twenty-four yearned for independence (J. Weinstein 1991, 252; E. Valenzuela 1984).

Privatization of health care and education, and changes in the administration of state funds, enlarged the discrepancy between services available to the wealthy and those available to the poor. Revenues from car license and business taxes, which formerly went to the central government now remained with the municipalities, with the consequence that "the poor had very meager resources to deal with overwhelming local needs" (Oppenheim 1993, 162).

Between 1980 and 1984, for example, the upper-class

districts of Santiago, Providencia and Las Condes, with 21 percent of Santiago's population, reported 56.8 percent of all municipal investment. The poor districts of La Granja, Cisterna, Conchali, and Pudahuel, with 36 percent of the population accounted for less than 9 percent of all municipal investment (Oppenheim 1993, 162).

In 1979, poor neighborhoods showed high rates of infant mortality, malnutrition, and poor health services, while wealthier neighborhoods showed the opposite, low rates of infant mortality, low levels of malnutrition, and high quality services (CED 1990, 107–117). In 1979, 21.36 percent of Santiago's wealthy lived in Las Condes, a neighborhood that housed only 6.78 of Santiago's population, including 1.1 percent of its most destitute, and 1.8 percent of its poor. La Pintana, by way of contrast, with 3.3 percent of Santiago's population housed 8.39 percent of Santiago's destitute, 5.13 percent of its poor, and only .65 percent of its wealthy (CED 1990, 136). While those living in La Pintana, La Granja, Cerro Navia, and Pudahuel lacked clean water, sewage systems, and utilities, and had less than a square meter of greenery for every inhabitant, those living in Las Condes or La Reina used the most clean water, the most electricity, had good sewage systems, and had more than 4 square meters of greenery per person (CED 1990, 80–83).

The privatization of the state increased the concentration of wealth in the hands of those families with access to liquid capital, while the poor were "systematically excluded and marginalized from the economic, political, and social decisions that affected them" (Valdes 1987, 20). In the social security arena, for example, policy makers maintained that the availability of multiple private firms competing for new members "would virtually assume the resources and the role of the state" (Stepan 1985, 323). Within one year of its creation, "70 percent of all social security and pension funds had been placed with only four AFP's (Administración de Fondos Previsionales [private pension funds]) controlled by two economic groups: Cruzat-Larraín and Javier Vial. . . . These forced savings from the workers—employer contributions to the plans stopped almost completely—constituted the largest single source of investment capital in the nation" (Volk 1983, 9).

In 1980, criticism from the Chilean church and international human-rights organizations grew. Again Pinochet responded with a plebiscite. The September 11, 1980, plebiscite on a new constitution was promoted as a referendum on democracy. The constitution, thus, contained a provision for a new plebiscite to be held in 1989, which would be followed by a free election if Pinochet lost. Alain Rouquie notes:

> In Latin America, the democratic regime has been and still remains more legitimate. . . . The military's need to justify its rule, to quell dissension within its ranks, and to gain international approval leads it to invoke the term democracy. . . . Even Pinochet, the most anti-liberal of all the dictators, found it necessary in both 1978 and 1980 to hold referenda which, while they justified the permanence in power of Pinochet himself also contained provisions for a return to civilian rule (Rouquie 1986, 111).

The 1980 plebiscite was far more important than the 1978 referendum, however, and represented more than a vote on Pinochet's continued rule. The 1980 Constitutional plebiscite was held to institutionalize the political and economic innovations that the military had, until then, imposed through brute force. At this, it was extremely successful.

On September 11, 68 percent of the voters approved the new constitution, 30 percent voted against it, and 2 percent spoiled their ballots. The vote gave Pinochet the facade of constitutionality that he needed so badly. The facade succeeded in large part because "the Constitution's key provisions were unknown to many who approved it" (Constable and Valenzuela 1986, 61). The writing was complicated, and no one was allowed to read the document until thirty days before the vote. As a leading partner at a prestigious Santiago law firm told Americas' Watch, "I supported the Constitution in 1980, but I made a mistake, I read it too quickly" (Americas' Watch 1988, 22).

None of the thirteen procedural guarantees that had been standard in Chilean elections were in effect. There were no voter registers, no protection against double voting, no political parties, and no poll watchers. "Even General Pinochet, when speaking of the 1978 consultation, acknowledged that at a bare minimum, a plebiscite requires an electoral law, electoral registration, designated voting sites, et cetera. None of these essential elements were in place in 1980" (Americas' Watch 1988, 20–22).

An analysis of the 1980 plebiscite reveals ample evidence of fraud (Bitar 1987, 8–9). Nationwide voter turnout seemed quite normal—of the 6,688,240 population over eighteen, 6,271,868 or 93.85 percent voted in the plebiscite—but when broken down by province, results were peculiar. For instance, in San Antonio, a traditional left-wing city with a population of 54,195; 56,230 voted in the plebiscite. Similarly, in Huasco, out of 32,970 eligible voters, 33,635 voted. This was repeated in Tocopilla, where 23,188 out of 22,167 eligible voters turned out at the polls, and in Cauquenes, where 158,772 of the eligible 152,344 voted. Summing the totals in the nine provinces where Pinochet had the strongest support, produced a 101.6 percent voter turnout (Bitar 1987, 8–9).

Fraud alone cannot explain the success of the 1980 plebiscite, however. Although the major producer groups in Chile, contrary to those in Uruguay, vigorously backed the regime, the economic elite had never captured majority support in Chile before (Stepan 1985, 326). Even the "manifestos in *El Mercurio* supporting the regime and exhorted the population to vote Yes" (González 1985, 17) is not enough to explain why the fraud failed to spark widespread opposition among middle-class groups, or why none of the Christian Democrat opposition leaders in Chile seriously challenged the plebiscite's legitimacy. If the opposition had denounced the fraud, or mobilized in protest, the plebiscite could have had a very different impact. Why was the opposition in 1980 so passive?

The victory of Pinochet's forces in the 1980 plebiscite, in sharp contrast to the opposition's victory in Uruguay during the same year, was the legacy of the political polarization preceding the coup in Chile. In Chile

> the center, at least the majority of the center, saw the fall of Allende as a liberation, and its participation in the events that culminated in the coup were decisive. . . . The Chilean congress (by condemning the government of Allende) invited the military to intervene, while the Uruguayan congress attempted to prevent it . . . the Uruguayan congress from the beginning refused to recognize the

legitimacy of the military regime, while the Chilean, conversely, contributed to the regime's legitimacy. . . . With the right and the left defined beforehand, the conduct of the center was crucial in both cases. In sum, to argue that the centrist electorate abandoned its leaders, is not, in Chile, an impartial manner to pose the question, because the electorate might feel that it was its political leaders who abandoned them. Between 1973 and 1980 it was the DC, not the electorate, that changed its course (González 1985, 19–20).

In 1973, Christian Democratic leaders had convinced middle-class voters that the political right and the military was their only protection against the Communist chaos. With the economic miracle still full of promise in 1980, and repression focused against the political left, the middle classes did not switch their allegiance. The left-wing parties hit hard by the repression could not risk protest and its certain repercussions without political allies.

The passage of the 1980 constitution had dramatic consequences for future political developments in Chile. The constitution consolidated Pinochet's personal power, giving him formal executive power and turning the military junta into a rubber stamp. Pinochet could both make and execute the law, while the junta could only approve legislation (or veto legislation by a unanimous vote in the junta, including the army general appointed by Pinochet). Pinochet assumed both the post of constitutional president and that of commander-in-chief of the armed forces. The constitution institutionalized Pinochet's rule, making the military's reconstruction of Chilean society almost immutable. The constitution also eliminated potential opposition, by allowing the progressive removal from the army of those high ranking officers who were Pinochet's peers at the time of the coup, . . . the concentration and centralization of the repressive apparatus under Pinochet's direct command, . . . [and] his personal control over the promotion mechanisms within the armed forces. . . . The September 1980 referendum and the March promulgation of the constitution marked a high point in the Pinochet regime's political institutionalization. . . . Previously visible tensions within the dominant bloc seemed to have been resolved in favor of Pinochet. . . . After the September plebiscite the opposition parties seemed impotent and disoriented (Garretón 1986, 111).

But if Pinochet's personal power was nearly absolute, civil society atomized, the middle classes passive, the poor overwhelmed with the daily requirements of survival, and the left nearly destroyed, how were protesters able to mount an offensive in 1983? What convinced urban shantytown residents to risk life and limb in the struggle against a regime they had so little chance of defeating?

CHAPTER FOUR

The Roots of Resistance

From 1973 to 1980, the military appeared invincible. It controlled neighborhoods through brute repression and factories through an economic model that made large sectors of the working class redundant. There was neither arena nor opportunity for protest. As James Scott observes "class conflict, like any other conflict, is played out on a site—the threshing floor, the assembly line, the place where piece-rates or rents are settled—where vital interests are at stake." Economic systems that "rely less on exploiting the poor directly, than on ignoring and replacing them . . . bulldoze the sites where conflict has historically occurred" (Scott 1985, 243). The unemployed are unable to threaten production, while the employed are constrained by the ease with which they can be replaced.

In authoritarian Chile, consistently high rates of unemployment, slightly masked by the government's two emergency work programs, made prospects for rebellion dim. By 1982, over 25 percent of the economically active population was unemployed or temporarily employed in government emergency work programs. Economic restructuring also increased the degree of social and economic fragmentation among the employed. While employment in industry dropped from 19 to 14 percent between 1973 and 1984, employment in commerce and services rose from 42 to 51 percent. Employment in the unprotected informal sector rose from 13.4 percent to 34 percent, and the number of street vendors doubled, from 58,000 to 105,400 in 1982 (Portes 1989, 30; Arellano 1987; Raczynski 1988). Women's labor-force participation also increased, rising from 27.6 percent of the total labor force in 1976 to 34.6 percent in 1985. Over 25 percent of women were employed in domestic service, while the remaining worked in the lowest wage, unorganized, sectors of the economy.

The reorganization of the economy reduced the size of natural collectivities and, in so doing, decreased the likelihood of spontaneous movements of the poor. With the labor unions and left-wing political parties decimated by repression, and their leadership dead or in exile, the poor were forced to rely on local forms of resistance that required little coordination. Scott observes, "The kinds of resistance and kinds of compliance we find . . . cannot be understood without reference to the larger context of real and anticipated coercion. . . . The coercive context creates and maintains the setting of relative powerlessness within which the dull compulsion of economic relations can extract its daily toll (Scott 1985, 278).

While they lacked the capacity to engage in open rebellion, left-wing activists continued to organize, silently bringing together those who shared grievances. If we classify activists in terms of the depth of their political commitment—"low loyalty" members are the least likely to engage in high risk actions, while "identifiers" are the most likely to do so. As individuals pass from a low level of loyalty, to a total identification with a collective, they shift the basis of their participation from one based on self-interest to one of total identification with the collective and willing self-sacrifice (Pizzorno 1993, 4). While repression may convince less loyal members to cease collective activity, identifiers will only leave when the organization "has become for him a different entity. He will leave when the identity of the organization is changed" (Pizzorno 1993, 4).

The first, and most risky, acts of resistance to the new regime, then, were organized by identifiers, those whose political affiliation was due "not to some specific end, but because in the collective reality of their political affiliation they received their own identity" (Pizzorno 1993, 4). Severed from contact with formal political networks and excluded from the traditional arenas of political action, activists relied on the informal social networks of religion, family, and neighborhood to recreate "the social and cultural space for the emergence of more favorable structural conditions conducive to collective actions" (A. D. Morris 1992, 371). Local parishes in left-wing shantytowns, in particular, became an attractive arena of resistance. The strength of the Catholic Church, as a national institution, and the accessibility of local parishes, particularly to women, facilitated reorganizing efforts around human rights. Indeed, within one year of the coup, new organizations such as the Agrupación de Mujeres Democráticas (Association of Democratic Women), the Agrupación de Familiares de Desaparecidos (Chilean Association of the Relatives of the Detained and Disappeared, formed in 1974), and the Agrupación de

Familiares de Presos Políticos, de Exiliados, y de Ejecutados (Association of Relatives of Political Prisoners, Relatives of Political Exiles, and Relatives of the Politically Executed, formed in 1975), were functioning openly (Chuchryk 1991, 156).

A second important arena of resistance to the dictatorship was the university. While university students had always been important political actors in Chile, the university took on particular importance in the dictatorship because of its atmosphere of intellectual debate in an otherwise repressively silent society. The university became the first site of open protest against the regime. While its semi-independent status allowed students a degree of resistance unavailable to other sectors of society, however, the university's isolation also increased its vulnerability to repression.

Ultimately, the most successful resistance efforts were in the poblaciones, in particular the traditional Communist poblaciones. The inability of left-wing activists to organize directly through elections, in Congress, in party headquarters, or union halls forced them to seek new forms of underground organizing. Popular organizations in left-wing shantytowns allowed the parties to escape their clandestine nuclei. As Manuel Castells describes a similar movement in Spain, "this alternative was basically a response to the immediate danger of police repression and relied on collective solidarity as a deterrent to institutional violence" (Castells 1983, 226).

Some analysts have suggested that the relationship between political parties and popular organizations is a competitive one; that the destruction of political parties during the dictatorship allowed popular organizations to grow (Oxhorn 1991, 1994). Yet in those neighborhoods where local party organizations were weak, popular organizations lacked direction. They did little more, in the words of one local activist, than "manage hunger." José Maravall cogently observes:

> The relationship between community factors and political parties in the generation of dissent has been a classic problem of political sociology. To what extent can political radicalism spread in a coherent and tightly knit proletarian community if political organizations are absent? And contrariwise, to what extent can political organizations attract support for radical programmes if there is no back-up in a solidaristic community? *Both factors must be interconnected in the genesis of political dissent under a dictatorship*: the underground groups were successful in those areas that were strong proletarian communities or in the protective milieu of universities, but at the same time the cultivation of the struggle was only possible where secret organizations were active (Maraval 1978, 166).

From 1973 through 1990, the resistance was strongest in the poblaciones where the Communist party had been traditionally active. In Christian Democratic poblaciones, individualism, competition, and fatalism crippled sporadic attempts at resistance. In traditional Socialist poblaciones, infighting among Socialist factions focused activists' energies inward. Where the MIR had been dominant residents had little experience in underground organizing. After the coup, MIR leaders fled the poblaciones, or were disappeared, leaving such poblaciones leaderless and vulnerable. The military savagely attacked Communist Party leaders too, disappearing hundreds and forcing the rest into exile. Yet grassroots activists, in poblaciones where the Communist

Party had previously been active, found it easier to reconstruct organizations of resistance. The Communist Party's work in the popular culture had created a network of experienced activists, a language and framework to interpret injustice, and a shared belief in the efficacy of collective action. As one noted sociologist observes, "It is difficult to construct from scratch. If people already share a sense of moral indignation and injustice, think of themselves as a we in opposition to some they, and have shared models of people like themselves acting to change conditions, the raw materials are in place" (Gamson 1992, 111).

The Church and Early Forms of Resistance

Initially, the Catholic Church was the only institution capable of confronting the regime. "All other major social organization in the country had been outlawed or placed under heavy surveillance or in recess, the church was the one remaining institution allowed to function openly" (B. H. Smith 1982, 289). Its tradition of conservatism, its opposition to the Unidad Popular, and its claim to represent large sectors of society made it a potentially powerful enemy for the new regime.

It was not at all certain, however, that the church would be willing to confront the new regime. Like its Argentine counterpart, the Chilean church initially avoided antagonistic relations with the military. On September 13, two days after the coup, the leaders of the Episcopal Conference praised the junta for its "patriotism and selflessness" (cited in B. H. Smith 1982, 288). In early October, the Archbishop

Fresno defended the coup, arguing that "the military did not perpetrate a fascist or brutal coup, but rather liberated the country" (B. H. Smith 1982, 292).

But the regime's increasingly brutal repression made political neutrality difficult for the priests and nuns working in the poblaciones, in particular those in the more activist neighborhoods. Confronted with the violence and brutality directed against many of their own parishioners, and challenged by the victim's families to defend them against the regime, many local nuns and priests became active human-rights advocates. The parishes opened their doors to those fleeing the military, offered solace to the families of those detained or disappeared, and provided activists a forum from which to condemn the escalating abuse.

The first to use the space provided by the local churches, to denounce and oppose the regime, predominantly, were women. Women were more likely to have connections with the local church and were, simultaneously, less likely to be targeted by the regime. "It was precisely women's traditional invisibility which allowed them to become political actors at a time when it was extremely dangerous for anyone else to do so," as one social scientist observes. "It was easier for women to work underground . . . because the military tended to ignore women" (Chuchryk 1991, 157).

The political parties, which had no other channels of political expression, discovered that their survival depended on the activities of these women. As María Elena Valenzuela observes: "The prohibition of partisan politics caused traditionally private arenas to become politicized. . . . The dividing line between public and private became blurred and the private arena, considered by some to be the exclusive domain of women, increasingly became a principal arena of conflict . . . leading to a virtual explosion of women's organizations" (M. E. Valenzuela 1991, 166).

In poblaciones with a history of grassroots activity, and strong intense grassroots networks, the local churches were more likely to be active against the regime. As one poblador in La Victoria, a población famous for the radical activism of the local church, explains, "Priests in our población have always been progressive because that is what we demand of them." The pobladores refuse to attend mass if the priest seems to prefer the rich. In 1963 the church appointed a conservative priest to the parish in La Victoria. The residents refused to accept him. Since then, María notes, "we have always had priests who worked with the población, fighting with us, never against us."

As local churches began to confront the dictatorship "many Christians stopped attending church," recalls Hugo Flores, president of Solidaridad. "Paralyzed by fear, they hid in their homes. Communists and other leftists, on the other hand, fled their homes and sought shelter in the church." The increased cooperation between the local church and local left-wing activists made local parishes extremely vulnerable.

In October 1973, Cardinal Silva Henríquez took steps to protect the local parishes. In cooperation with representatives of Methodist, Lutheran, and other Protestant churches, as well as the Jewish community, he created the Comité de Cooperación para la Paz en Chile (COPACHI, the Committee of Cooperation for Peace), to coordinate the human-rights work of the myriad local parishes. Cardinal Heníquez gave COPACHI the full backing of the Catholic Church, and in so doing brought the church hierarchy directly into the political arena.

> By working on a daily basis with those suffering the consequences of repression, priests and nuns in low-income areas were exposed more directly to the consequences of repression than the hierarchy. Though not in a position to exercise the same type of public influence as the bishops, they acted as a constant source of pressure on the prelates to speak and act more critically against the government. While such suggestions were not always heeded by the bishops, the flow of information and criticisms continued to move up the vertical chain of command in the Church throughout the period of consolidation of the regime's power (B. H. Smith 1982, 314–315).

By August 1974, COPACHI had 104 full-time employees (up from eight in November) in Santiago alone. By 1975 this number had more than doubled, and COPACHI commanded a national network of over three hundred full-time lawyers, social workers, and medical personnel (Frühling 1984, 356). As one human-rights lawyer notes, "the Committee had become the center around which the relatives of those who were detained—and later, beginning in 1975, disappeared— began to organize themselves. These were the first public organizations formed by people so close to the victims of repression, and this certainly was evidence of a revival of the will to oppose the regime" (Frühling 1984, 363).

On November 11, 1975, Pinochet forced the cardinal to dissolve the Committee. There was an immediate outcry from the human-rights community. The following month the cardinal replaced COPACHI with the Vicaría de

Solidaridad. Except for its even closer affiliation with the church, the Vicaría was almost an identical replica of the organization the government had banned. "The strategy of the cardinal was shrewd and farsighted. The new Vicariate of Solidarity was more closely tied to the Church than its predecessor, making it both easier for the bishops to control and harder for the government to attack without directly attacking the core of the church itself" (B. H. Smith 1982, 318).

The Vicaría soon established regional offices in twenty of the twenty-five provinces. By 1977 it was providing fifty thousand political prisoners with legal support and thirty thousand of the economically destitute with food and shelter. The Vicaría also provided psychological treatment that enabled political prisoners to return to work. The Vicaría's prestige and close identification with the church enabled it to employ prominent Christian Democratic lawyers, physicians and professionals who had been active opponents of the Unidad Popular. It thus forged "human and political bonds among people who were slowly to become part of the opposition" (Frühling 1984, 360).

In 1977, the association of Catholic bishops issued a declaration at the Episcopal Conference, openly attacking the legitimacy of the military regime. The document argued:

> The actions which we denounce and condemn are not isolated incidents. They are part of an overall process or system that is very clearly delineated in its characteristics and which threatens to impose itself relentlessly throughout Latin America. By a constant appeal to National Security, a model of society is being consolidated that takes away basic liberties, runs roughshod over the most fundamental rights and subjugates citizens to a dreaded and omnipotent police state.

The church cannot remain passive or neutral in face of such a situation. The legacy which it has received from Christ demands that it speak out in favor of human dignity and for the effective protection of liberty and the rights of person (José Manuel Santos 1976, 597–599, cited in B. H. Smith 1982, 307).

By 1978, the cooperation between the church and the left-wing parties had facilitated the reemergence of political activity in shantytowns, union halls, and universities. The church's importance as an arena of opposition was now superseded by the revival of grassroots political activity:

> The Church cannot undermine states or alter their political economy . . . but [it] has staying power and is not easily smashed . . . The organizational network of the church, therefore, can act as an important holding operation or locus of minimal resistance until other forms of domestic and international pressure can be mobilized. It cannot by itself, however, act as an effective front line of major opposition to authoritarian regimes (B. H. Smith 1982, 350).

After 1978 the Church continued to play the role it had assumed following the coup—a shelter for victims of human rights abuse and an arena in which the poor and oppressed could gather and articulate political demands.

The Student Movement

Like churches, universities are a natural site for dissent in an authoritarian regime. It is difficult for an authoritarian regime to completely repress them without destroying the intellectual life that makes education possible. Yet, if the regime allows academic life to flourish, universities become the only open arena of discussion and dissent in an otherwise closed society. It is this paradox that pushes the university into the forefront of resistance to authoritarian rule.

In Chile, the universities were the first sites of open rebellion. At the Pedagógico (Teachers College) of the Universidad de Chile, mass protests shook the campus four years before those that shook the nation. Patricia Torres, a student leader at the Pedagógico explains:

> Despite the use of extreme forms of repression against both students and faculty, the government could not eliminate all left-wing students. In 1973 there were too many students with a great deal of political experience. They knew what student life had been like before the coup. They had come from families that participated in the Unidad Popular, or they had organized during the Unidad Popular, themselves, but were not well known.

After the coup, these young activists began to regroup. The climate in the university was very tense. Since the military administered the campuses, students could not organize openly. The government had dismissed over two thousand professors and expelled over twenty thousand students at the time of the coup. By 1983 "it was estimated that a university system that accommodated one hundred forty thousand students in 1973 would serve only twenty thousand by 1985," notes Chuchryk (Chuchryk 1991, 162). Since the university did not provide on-campus housing, students were together on campus for very short periods. Organizing in this context required patience and imagination. "We tried to rebuild communication networks, to create new forms of organization," Torres explains. "We got together after class. Sometimes we organized research and study groups where students could begin to speak about issues. We also organized at parties, and sports events, even football games. Gradually we began to reconstruct networks of communication."

The Communists were most active in this style of organizing. They created cultural workshops to revive collective identities and to regenerate the culture of the Unidad Popular, with its New Song Movement, mural artistry, and poetry. They also used the cultural workshops to discuss political and social inequities. In photography workshops, for instance, students displayed photos of the misery and homelessness. Students in poetry workshops read poems by Pablo Neruda, such as the "Cantata de Iquique," about the massacre of nitrate miners in 1907. In music workshops students rehearsed songs written by Violeta Parra and Victor Jara about the popular movements of the sixties and early seventies. In art clubs they painted murals reminiscent of those painted by the Communist Ramona Parra Brigade.

Until 1976, these resistance efforts were clandestine and included only left-wing activists, since the Christian Democrats were still ambivalent toward the new regime. The Universidad de Chile's 1976 tuition policy, however, forced students to assume educational expenses previously guaranteed by the state and brought Christian Democratic students into the struggle. Tuition policy became a rallying point. The Christian Democratic Youth began to form committees on tuition and debt. The committees drew Christian Democratic students into closer collaboration with Communists and the Communist culture clubs. The

Pedagógico which had the largest percentage of working-class students and was not as severely repressed as the former Universidad Técnica, became the heart of the student movement.

In 1978, the cultural clubs at the Pedagógico merged to form the Agrupación Cultural Universitaria (ACU, University Cultural Association). Simultaneously, the Christian Democratic led Comités de Participación (Committees of Participation), themselves an outgrowth of the tuition workshops, united to form the Coalition of Committees of Participation. The coalition began to work in the cultural arena, coordinating activities and fund-raisers with the ACU. Soon, Ricardo Brodsky and Ramiro Pizarro observe:

> New student organizations began to sprout like mushrooms—cultural workshops, committees on economic problems. . . . The Committees of Participation were only comparable to the ACU in importance. These were our two institutions—with them we could return to the public arena; we [political activists] could escape the clandestinity where the regime had cornered us (Brodsky and Pizarro 1985, 141).

By 1978, the movement had taken an overtly political tone. Activities that "had begun as cultural, or issue oriented activities, now ended with political slogans" (Torres). On September 11, 1978, the Coalition of Committees of Participation and the ACU held a public assembly in the name of the disappeared. "There was no question as to the political implications of this act," notes Torres. It was the first truly political act." After the assembly, the military expelled two students, Rodolfo Fortunate (Christian Democrat) and Carlos Pérez (Communist), from the university.

The expulsion of Fortunate and Pérez marked the beginning of a pattern of selective repression against the more activist students. The repression forced the students to overcome ideological and sectarian divisions. "Since the police did not ask us our ideology, they made us equal," insist Brodsky and Pizarro (Brodsky and Pizarro, 1985, 142).

In 1979, the regime responded to the growing movement by creating its own student organization—the Federación de Centros de Estudiantes de Chile (FECECH, Student Federation of the University of Chile). It structured the FECECH to diffuse the student movement by allowing students to democratically elect their own delegates to an advisory board, called the Consejo Facultad, whose members would select the president of the FECECH.

The intention was to depoliticize student elections by narrowing the range of candidates to those in one's own department. If the opposition was unable to present a winning candidate in each department and win at least 50 percent of the delegates, the progovernment students would control the student assembly. The outgoing student assembly would then retain voting power on the Consejo Facultad in the next student election.

The creation of the FECECH confronted students with a dilemma. "If we participated, we might legitimize the dictatorship's organization. If we didn't participate, we might miss an opportunity to create a genuine democratic space from within," explains Torres. Christian Democrats supported participation, the MIR rejected it. The Communists, after deliberation, decided to use the FECECH to rebuild the student movement, "to participate, to democratize" (Torres).

In March 1979, elections to the FECECH were held. On

most campuses of the Universidad de Chile the opposition forces were hopelessly fragmented, and the government maintained control over the new student assembly. In the Pedagógico the opposition won over 50 percent of the delegates on the first ballot. "This defeated the government's strategy," explains Torres, "they had not thought that we could win on the first ballot."

The Christian Democrats won the majority, and with it, the presidency. The Communists, with the second largest plurality, won the vice-presidency. The Socialists came in third, and a Socialist was appointed secretary. The Christian Left, in fourth place, were given the post of treasurer. Not anticipating such an early sweep, the student's success threw the government off guard. Students had used the government's attempt to coopt the movement to reclaim the democratic spaces closed by the coup.

After the FECECH elections, the students began to address issues beyond the scope of the university. On May 1, 1979, they joined a massive labor rally. The following month they called for a strike in the Spanish department in solidarity with a professor, whose son had disappeared, and who, herself, had been fired. The students paralyzed the college for three days. In retaliation, the administration expelled forty-nine students. "Afterwards," explains Torres, "we began to work in solidarity with those who had been expelled." The confrontations between students and the military became increasingly violent.

Inside the university itself, the military increased its operations, torturing, arresting, and internally exiling the student activists. Forty students, including Torres, were arrested, tortured, and "relegated" to distant parts of the country. Hundreds more were expelled. The armed forces

OSCAR SÁEZ

A 1979 student demonstration at the Pedagógico of the Universidad de Chile.

began to control the doors of the university to prevent the expelled students from entering the campus. It forbade student delegates who had been active in 1979 to register in 1980, unless they signed documents promising not to participate in any student activities.

The students responded to the new regulations with offensive actions. They threw rocks and eggs at the guards and police and physically attacked suspected informants within the university. The high level of political violence provoked a tension within the movement; should the movement aim to broaden its support base or should students try to intensify the struggle? If the student leaders hoped to reach broader sectors of the student body they would have to "change their form of struggle." If they chose to maintain the current rhythm and intensity of struggle (and with it, the employment of directed violence), they would have to sacrifice the opportunity to incorporate larger sectors of the student body (Brodsky and Pizarro 1985, 147).

Convinced that the movement could not succeed without the support of the bulk of the student body, the student leaders opted to change the form of struggle. They transformed the campus into an open, permanent public assembly, encouraging the participation of all the students on campus. The generalized atmosphere of rebellion culminated in a general strike in November 1980. Torres notes:

> The strike was supported by secondary strikes in the colleges of Philosophy and Letters, Education, Science and Humanities. Over fifteen thousand students participated. Classes were suspended, and pitched battles raged between students and police. The authorities began to take much more forceful measures. They expelled another thirty-nine students. They also began to arrest students when they were outside the university, to torture and internally exile them.

The students responded with a massive hunger strike. Finally the administration moved to negotiate, but the conversations with the authorities divided the movement. How should the students respond to concessions offered by the administration? "Should they accept the limited nature of the concessions offered, using the mobilizations to achieve limited goals, or should they pursue a maximalist strategy, prolonging the mobilization indefinitely, risking everything in the struggle against the dictatorship" (Torres)?

The issue struck at the heart of the movement. Was it worth risking students lives to win concessions that only would affect a few students at the Pedagógico? Yet, how could one small isolated university student movement defeat a military dictatorship? In the end, the question was moot. In 1981 the government simply closed the Pedagógico, and replaced it with the Universidad Metropolitana (Metropolitan University), a professional academy under a level of "police vigilance more appropriate to a concentration camp than a university," observe Brodsky and Pizarro (1985, 148). Torres notes:

> They hit us very hard. Nineteen eighty-one marked a new stage in the development of the student movement. Many students were left with a high degree of pessimism. The mobilization died out. The panorama changed entirely. Looking back, it seems we developed too rapidly during this period, we were ahead of everyone else. It was necessary to wait for other sectors that could work with us. This we learned through experience.

Indeed the struggle at the Pedagógico in many ways foreshadowed the larger movement to come. Like the movement that emerged in 1983, its strength grew out of informal solidary networks, forged in earlier struggles. Grassroots activists revitalized these networks by bringing together those who shared grievances and by organizing activities that revived collective historical memories. As Torres notes, the struggle during this phase "was a united one, despite ideological differences and divergent views" (Torres).

After 1983, the student movement would have access to

more formal resources. The reemergence of national political parties would extend the movement throughout the nation. National student federations would reemerge and the student movement would be absorbed into an increasingly political national protest movement. This, however, is the subject of chapter five.

Labor Unions

While students were organizing political opposition in the universities, grassroots labor activists were attempting to retake control of the union base. Such efforts were among the most dangerous of the period. Several contingent factors made labor organizing particularly difficult. First, the regime was especially vigilant of the labor unions. Those suspected of organizing against the regime were subject to arrest, torture, or even death. Organizers who survived the repression were fired and blacklisted. Ana recalls:

> After the coup, I was afraid to return to the factory. The military had seized twelve workers there—eleven Communists and one Christian Democrat. They were never seen again. Later another friend of mine, Pedro Rojas, was arrested and tortured to death. A worker at the factory queried the foreman about why I had been allowed to stay. The foreman argued that since I was pregnant he could not fire me. My husband no longer had a job, and I had child at home.

Second, the size of the industrial population was drastically reduced by the new economic model. The traditional left-wing strongholds such as textiles, mining (except copper), and construction were the most dramatically affected. By 1981 the percentage of unionized workers had declined from an average of 41 percent of the labor force in 1972, to less than 10 percent (Ruiz-Tagle 1985). With poverty affecting 36 percent of the population in 1978 (up from 28.5% in 1969), unemployment running close to 20 percent (discounting emergency employment programs for those inscribed on government lists), and new employment opportunities concentrated in the low-wage, unorganized-service sector, strike activity was unlikely to succeed.

Third, the political parties most closely connected with the labor movement had been destroyed or forced underground. The Socialist Party, in particular, was unprepared to resist the military onslaught. "Its lack of internal discipline, and the ideological debates that had always dominated its functioning had devastating effects," notes Carmelo Furci. "Its militants were isolated, no political directives were available . . . and the disintegration of the party's organization was almost complete" (Furci 1984, 141). The Communist Party had also lost most of its leaders, and its internal communication networks were seriously marred. Few of the MIR's activists had even survived the first two years of the dictatorship, and the other smaller left-wing parties had all but disappeared. The Christian Democrats simply ceased political activity.

But the economic hardship endured by factory workers, combined with the legal restrictions on union activity, "reinforced the need of the unions to seek external support from the parties, politicized rather than depoliticized union action" (Angell 1991, 194). José, a Communist labor organizer, remembers:

> We [grassroots activists] began working clandestinely in
> the factories, trying to reestablish underground unions.
> We began by organizing youth activities, as early as 1974.
> By 1975 we had created illegal union federations, and
> interfederations, and youth sections within each federation.

On May 1, 1975, the illegal federations designated a
national coordinating body. In October of the same year,
the *coordinador* sent a letter to the cardinal asking him to
intercede with the government on behalf of the rapidly
deteriorating situation of organized labor. A year later the
coordinador was transformed into a permanent organization called the Coordinador Nacional Sindical (CNS, National Union Confederation), a national union confederation
uniting construction, mining, industrial, and agricultural
unions. In the same year a different group of union leaders,
representing public sector workers formed the Grupo de
Diez (Group of Ten)."

On May 1, 1976, young Communists, Socialists, MAPU,
Left Christian, and MIR activists within the union movement, organized a theatrical event in honor of May day.
Over four thousand attended. After the play all of the
organizers were sought by the police. Those who were
found were disappeared. The government also disappeared
twenty-seven leaders of the Communist Party and the Communist Youth during this period. Surviving left-wing labor
organizers fled to the poblaciones. José, for instance, did
not return to the union halls until 1978.

Between 1976 and 1978, only the copper miners at El
Teniente, the largest copper mine, could maintain some
degree of labor militancy. Despite government intervention in the Confederación de Cobre (CTC, Copper Miners

Confederation), in November of 1977, the miners called an illegal strike. The government dismissed seventy miners and arrested the four leaders who they exiled to remote parts of the country (Falabella 1989, 229).

In 1978, the government created the Unión Nacional de Trabajadores Chilenos (UNTRACH, National Union of Chilean Workers), a progovernment alternative to the illegal CNS and Grupo de Diez. In response the two illegal union confederations signed a new accord and on May 1, 1978, called an act of celebration. The government responded by issuing Decree Law 2200, overriding the labor rights contained in the traditional labor code. The Grupo de Diez issued a joint declaration of protest with the U.S. American Federation of Labor–Congress of Industrial Organizations (AFL– CIO), and the CNS published a similar declaration with the Frente Unitario Trabajador (FUT, United Workers Front) and the Confederación Latinoamericana de Trabajadores (CLAT, Confederation of Latin American Workers). At El Teniente, miners refused to enter the dining room at lunch hour, a protest known as the *viandazo* (Falabella 1989, 230). The government responded by dissolving seven of the federations affiliated with the CNS, taking stern measures sagainst public employees associated with the Grupo de Diez, and threatening union leaders with arrest.

The repression against Chilean labor spurred the AFL– CIO to declare an international boycott of Chilean produce. The CNS, FUT, and the Confederación de Empleados Particulares de Chile (CEPCH, the union of white-collar employees), a group of federations that had abandoned the Grupo de Diez, argued that the situation demanded the formation of a united union movement (Falabella 1989, 220).

In January 1979, the government announced a new labor code. The code eliminated restrictions on union meetings and called for elections in most sectors of the private economy. Persons who had been union leaders, or who had known affiliation with political parties over the past ten years, were excluded from eligibility for new union leadership positions. It also proscribed candidacies before the election. This was a direct attempt to replace the union leaders who had become oppositional. Strikes were limited to sixty days, although companies could hire new workers after thirty, and collective bargaining could only occur at the plant level (Chuchryk 1991, 152).

Several unintended consequences, however, resulted from the new laws.

1. They gave organizers the opportunity to discuss political issues with the rank-and-file.

2. They allowed parties with strong underground networks to take advantage of the dispersion of votes by independent workers, increasing the probability that their preferred candidates would be elected.

3. They allowed workers to replace union leaders who had held power since the coup with even older, more experienced, left-wing activists.

4. The new code legalized strike activity (although it restricted the length of a strike to sixty days, and permitted management to freely replace striking workers), and in so doing revitalized the labor movement.

Within months of the new legislation, labor leaders had stepped up pressure on the government and were leading demonstrations in Santiago and Valparaiso. On May 1, 1979, university students, human-rights organizers, and political militants joined labor leaders in the largest mass demonstration since the coup. Over three hundred protesters were arrested.

In 1980, miners at El Teniente struck for forty-four days. At the end of the forty-four day period the CTC, under the leadership of Rodolfo Seguel, dropped its demands for a 10 to 16 percent increase in real wages and settled for an increase of 2 percent in 1981 and 1 percent in 1982 (Investor Responsibility Research Center, Washington D.C., March 18, 1981).

On May 1, 1980, labor leaders again called for a mass rally in downtown Santiago. The government responded with threats of violence, and the rally was small. Fifty-two of the protesters were arrested. The unions were still too weak to resist the government's attacks. As one Communist militant explained, "It's true that we can count on a great deal of strength among the working class, but this class fights in the poblaciones, not in the factories. In the factories we have been unable to reestablish ourselves firmly because of the effects of fierce repression, fear of unemployment, and because of the threats" (Lozza 1986, 16).

Resistance in the Poblaciones

By 1982, over 1.3 million people were living in Santiago's slums and shantytowns. Organizing in such areas was extremely difficult. Shantytowns had always been more heterogeneous than factories or universities. Dramatic drops in industrial production increased that diversity, while it simultaneously reduced the residents' economic leverage. Long standing political and ideological conflicts often exacerbated status and occupational differences. Making the

situation even more difficult, was the high percentage of
población residents under thirty. Most of them lacked political experience and knew little of life before the dictatorship.

Yet, there were also large differences between
poblaciones. Those created by government programs such
as Operación Sitio, or settled randomly by drifters tended
to have weak grassroots networks and little capacity to
resist the dictatorship. Residents in such neighborhoods, as
Las Parcelas and Remodelación, for example, struggled
silently and alone. They avoided political activists and
dreamed of the day they or their children could move out of
poverty.

In those poblaciones that had been a result of illegal
land takeovers organized by the MIR or Socialists in the late
1960s and early seventies, grassroots networks were fragile.
Activists who tried to organize in these poblaciones, or the
more radical sectors of such large poblaciones as Lo
Hermida, Villa O'Higgens, and Sara Gajardo, were often
defenseless against military repression. Many managed to
assemble enough activists to create popular organizations,
but the less political residents refused to participate. As
Nelson observes, "those who acted publicly knew they were
as good as dead, there were just too many informants."

In poblaciones with a long history of collective action
and close association with the Communist Party, such as La
Victoria, Pablo Neruda, Herminda de la Victoria, Yungay,
and Granadilla, grassroots activists created new forms of
popular resistance by organizing around community needs.
"Success in overcoming dilemmas of collective action and
the self-defeating opportunism that they spawn depends on
the broader social context within which any particular game
is played. Voluntary cooperation is easier in a community

that has inherited a substantial stock of human capital in the form of reciprocity and networks of civil engagement" (Putnam 1993, 167).

In both Las Parcelas and Lo Hermida, fear and distrust prevented activists from reaching out to potential new members. In contrast, local grassroots networks in Yungay, Herminda de la Victoria, and Granadilla, allowed the more traditional political activists to recruit new militants, and work in new arenas such as private homes, churches, and soup kitchens. The distinction between the organizing style and experience of activists in Las Parcelas and Lo Hermida, on the one hand, and Yungay, Herminda de la Victoria, and Granadilla, on the other, is revealing.

Poblaciones with Weak Horizontal Networks

LAS PARCELAS

Las Parcelas is a población settled randomly at first, and later by patrons of Operación Sitio. Political activists who began to organize in the seventies, helped residents gain essential city services. There was little correspondence between the discourse and ideology of these political activists, however, and the culture of this community. After the coup, this schism became a serious liability. The military wrested control of the neighborhood council, routed out the activists, and dismantled all remaining popular organizations. Leo, a local Communist organizer observes:

> From 1973 until 1978 we were alone. We had to do everything alone—playing several roles at once. Many men

were broken by fear. Others shut their doors, out of terror, this terrible terror that we had never known.

Some activists sought protection from the local church. "The church had an aura of respectability," Leo explains. "The military repressed it, but they respected it." Under the church's protective auspices, organizations of human rights began to appear. Many human rights activists were killed, however, and even the priests were persecuted. Leo recalls:

We tried to protect party leaders during this period, but it was very difficult. We tried to disguise our meetings, getting together under the pretext of baptisms, birthdays, weddings, or anniversaries. But the Communists in this neighborhood were very well known. In 1974 the military arrested five Communist Party leaders. All five were disappeared.

"As the terror grew," notes Leo, "a huge number of political activists ceased political work altogether. There were so few of us, and we were mostly youngsters." The more committed activists began to work in neighboring poblaciones where they were less likely to be recognized. Leo, for instance, began to work in Lo Hermida, at the base of the mountain, a población with a more radical past. There, argues Leo,

we accomplished things that are hard to believe today. Mostly political agitation—distributing pamphlets and propaganda, painting graffiti, et cetera. For example, one night we painted slogans on all the walls in Lo Hermida. All night long we put up posters. It made us laugh. We thought people must be saying what a huge quantity of Communists there must be here. This was the propaganda part of the work. To work in the social organizations was much more difficult. We were afraid of being found out.

They began to create new organizations under the protection of the church. They formed organizations for the unemployed (*bolsas de cesantes*), workshops for carpenters and other skilled workers (*talleres*), and, after the flood, soup kitchens (*ollas comunes*), and social organizations with entirely new members. Most of those who joined these organizations were political activists. Leo admits:

> I think there were very few involved who weren't activists from one party or another—Socialists, Christian Democrats, Left Christians, MAPU, or ourselves. With all the organizations that we had—talleres, bolsas de cesantes, et cetera—we had about a thousand people organized in a población of seventy thousand. The vast majority were not involved. We reached some with agitation and propaganda, but we could not get them involved in social organizations. They were simply terrified. And we didn't have the political know-how to win them. We avoided the social organizations that the residents joined—the sports clubs, the neighborhood councils, the mothers' centers—we left them to the dictatorship.

And Nelson, a young organizer concurs:

> Before I became political, I had been active in the neighborhood sports club. After I joined the Communist Party, I was told to abandon the sports club and instead create a human-rights group. I was removed from an organization

with over two hundred members to create a Committee of Human Rights with less than twelve. We could not convince anyone here to work with us because we were marked politically, it was simply too risky.

In Las Parcelas and Lo Hermida, political activists felt isolated and vulnerable. Their isolation limited their political work. Granovetter has argued that weak ties are often more important than strong ties in mobilizing communities (Granovetter 1973), since individuals are in loose contact with people they do not know, while in communities with strong intense ties, competition and fragmentation may weaken grassroots efforts (Granovetter 1973, 1371).

Under conditions of intense repression, however, strong networks are needed to motivate residents to risk their lives in protest. In Chile, residents who lived in communities with weak ties were fatalistic about the future and lacked confidence in themselves. "Residents won't participate," notes Leo. "If we try to initiate activities, the residents just watch us, they don't participate." Like those in the southern Italian neighborhoods, observed by Putnam, "people in these communities felt powerless and exploited" (Putnam 1993, 182).

Poblaciones with Strong Grassroots Networks

In poblaciones with a history of grassroots activity and strong intense grassroots networks, early organizing activities were far more successful, and activists were able to enlist more support from passive or disconnected members of the community.

HERMINDA DE LA VICTORIA

Like many of the more combative poblaciones, Herminda was settled illegally by the Communist Party's Committee of the Homeless. The occupation of Herminda in 1967, was met with severe police repression. The población was roped in by police forces and virtually under siege for nine months. During the siege, a baby girl took ill and, unable to reach a hospital, died. The población was named Herminda in her honor.

Finally, an agreement was reached with the government. The occupants were transported to a vacant area, named Herminda de la Victoria, and were sold rights to the land. The residents were given 45 hectares for 1,464 families, and asked to sign a contract requiring that they pay on a sliding scale. After three years the new occupants were to hold the deeds to their homes. The government through CORVI, was to provide water and sanitary services.

The 1973 coup hit the población very hard, but by 1974 the residents of Herminda began to reorganize under the protection of the Church. "We began with about twenty families," recalls Violeta. The first social organization they created was a health-care center. Later they created a human-rights committee. Violeta recalls that

perhaps four in twenty from this población were active, the rest were terrified. Those of us who were active were all members of political parties, of course. I'm a Socialist, but I worked with the Communists, Miristas, and Left Christians, as well. I think it was easier to organize in Herminda, since we had all known each other, worked together for so many years, since the "toma" [illegal land seizure]. We knew who was who. It was difficult for informants to work in this neighborhood, since we identified them right away. Consequently, Herminda became a center of resistance activity. Residents of all the neighboring poblaciones came here to organize.

In 1979, Juan Araya, the ex-president of the Committee of the Homeless, and the Metropolitana de Pobladores (the población coordinating organization linked to the Communist Party) began a series of meetings in Herminda. The Church-linked Agrupacíon Vecinal, Organization of Neighbors (AVEC) also participated. They decided to demand that the regime respect the 1967 contract giving residents of Herminda deeds to their homes.

The meetings became the basis of the Committee of Pobladores, which led the struggle to reclaim the rights granted in the original housing contract. A member of the Committee said:

> We pointed to a clause in the contract that guaranteed that all pre-1976 agreements be honored. The government responded with threats. The residents of the población Viña began to gather to defend us. They held meetings with lawyers. The first week forty attended, the second week two hundred attended, the third week five hundred attended. Then there were no more meetings. We gathered in front of the official neighborhood council to denounce them. They responded with extreme repression, attempting to eliminate the Committee of Pobladores. The secret police threatened the leaders of the committee with arrest or even death.
>
> We had, however, our ideas very clear, and we simply continued. The official press launched a campaign against

us. The secret police began an investigation and followed up with threats. The carabineros surrounded the church and the Christian community. But the residents of the community responded en masse and continued to meet every Sunday. If the police or secret police tried to single out one of us for punishment, the rest of the población responded, and made it impossible for the police to arrest or disappear only one of us.

Finally, in April 1980, the government gave in. Ninety five percent of Herminda de la Victoria's residents were given the deeds to their homes. The official neighborhood council resigned in embarrassment. The municipality was obliged to call for free elections. "Ninety five percent of the población voted for us," exclaims Pablo, an ex-member of the democratic council. Through community participation and solidarity, the población was able to resist the regime's repression and reclaim housing rights. But the community did not cease political activity once housing claims had been satisfied, however. They demanded recognition of their democratically elected neighborhood council as well. They became the first community in Santiago to reestablish democratic self-government. As Pablo, explains:

> Pedro was voted president. He and I were the only two in the junta that were not Communists. We were elected in June 1980. On December 25, 1980, we held a Christmas festival to celebrate our victory. Two thousand five hundred children participated. All of the pobladores contributed something.
> On the 16th of March we celebrated our anniversary. Everyone participated. We invited people to dance in the streets, to join in parades.

YUNGAY

Yungay, originally known as Villa Lenin, was settled in October 1971 as a result of an agreement between the government housing authority and the Communist Committee of the Homeless. It was financed by a grant from the Banco de Desarrollo (International Development Bank), as part of an international aid package from the Soviet Union. The población was to be a model development for the Socialist government of Salvador Allende. The first eighteen hundred families settled in the población were carefully screened. Those most committed to the success of the new socialist community were the first resettled.

On October 6, 1973, three weeks after the coup three Communist and Socialist leaders of the neighborhood council of Villa Lenin (renamed Villa Esmerelda by the military, but called Yungay by most residents) sought an audience with the governor of Santiago. They told him that they were leaders of the población Villa Lenin, and that they wished to present themselves to the authorities and to provide them with a list of all the members of the población. They argued that the military had seized the buildings constructed for the members of the población, forcing pobladores to remain in the shacks that had been designated as temporary housing. They asked the government to provide a solution.

The población leaders left political activists off the list of población residents, listing their wives as single women, and did not mention their own political affiliation. Instead, they stressed their identification with the población, and the desperate plight of its residents. Victor Molina, the president of the neighborhood council at the time of the coup explains:

Our población was among the least repressed in Santiago, despite its fame as a Communist center. We had Communist leaders from all over the country hidden here. But the authorities never raided the población. In part, because unlike other población leaders, we never fled, so the military had no excuse to search for us. The other part was the solidarity we felt with the residents. No one here informed the police of political activity. Consequently no población residents were killed during the first ten years of the dictatorship.

Similarly, a local priest observes, the maturity of the political activists in Yungay and their deep roots in the población facilitated understanding between political activists and the Christian community: "There is more participation from the base in both the political parties and in the Christian community. There is more cross-membership, more linkages between members, more people who participate in both organizations."

In 1974, several Communist leaders created a sports club for young pobladores called Juventud Latina. Later they created a soup kitchen under church auspices, and then women's workshops. As Irma, a Christian Democratic organizer in Yungay, recalls:

Women were the first to become political here. We understood the situation better than the men, because we had to feed our children. We had to explain to our children why there was no food. So, we created soup kitchens to feed our children. But, when we began to get involved, we were exposed to the regime's repression. A woman arrived, for instance, and told us that her son went out one day and that she later found his body tortured and bullet

CATHY LISA SCHNEIDER

Children in Yungay pretending to be combatants in the Frente Patriótico Manuel Rodríguez, 1986.

ridden in the canal. The regime also began to attack organizers, forcing us to form new organizations for self-protection. In this way, we learned to depend on each other.

In 1978, they created the first Communist cell, which then led the battle to reclaim the building seized by the military. They won new apartment buildings for all of the población's residents in 1979. Later that year they formed two more Communist cells. In 1980 they created a Comité Pro Retorno, to help political exiles. The Pro Retorno committee evolved into a committee of human rights (*comité de derechos humanos*), which was made up of three Communists, three Christian Democrats, a Socialist, and an independent (Ana was elected president of the committee). As Irma, the Christian Democratic organizer, recalls:

I did not see it at the time, but it's clear to me now that all the people with whom I worked were political activists. Most of them were Communists. Ana used to invite me to participate in women's workshops and soup kitchens. "We all share the same problems," she said. "It doesn't matter ·where you participate or with whom, just get involved." It was through Ana, that I began to understand why I was hungry, why my husband was unemployed. I began to realize that the government had a great deal to do with the situation in which I was living. My husband, on the other hand, still does not understand it, though our son is a political prisoner.

By 1982, Yungay boasted a neighborhood cooperative (*comprando juntos*), a women's center, and a health center. By 1983 it had one of the first democratically elected neighborhood councils.

GRANADILLA

Granadilla, in Valparaiso, followed a trajectory similar to that followed in Yungay and Herminda. Granadilla was settled in 1971, when grassroots Communist activists defied party orders and illegally seized a plot of land promised by the outgoing government. As Chino, the president of the neighborhood council of Granadilla, recalls, "political activists in this población always put the población before the party."

In contrast to Las Parcelas or Lo Hermida, where political militants were forced to flee mass organizations for fear of being found out, in Granadilla, the first act of resistance was the building of a collective farm on the edge of the mountain in 1974. The farm became the basis for a communal kitchen. In January of 1975 members of the communal kitchen created *Chile Joven* (Young Chile), to organize the youth. By 1976 Chile Joven was sponsoring cultural activities, *peñas* (coffee houses), folk concerts, and theater. Chino notes that

> from that time on we worked, not only to resolve the problem of hunger, but to organize the población in its entirety. We began to bring together people who had nothing to do with politics, they came to eat. When one confronts a problem like hunger, everyone is political, so we created a community kitchen. It was only later that we created the party. We always had the residents behind us, not just a particular political party. It was very difficult to attack us, since we interpreted the desires of the people, and the people were part of us.

This flexibility allowed Granadilla to resolve the endemic problem of unemployment, which in poblaciones like Granadilla sometimes exceeded seventy percent. Most of Granadilla's residents depended on government emergency employment programs for survival. The local official who administered the programs, however, lacked imagination. Those inscribed in the program were forced to pursue menial, pointless tasks, such as sweeping the central plaza in the center of the wealthy suburb Viña del Mar. Eventually the mayor began to receive a lot of criticism. Chino remembers:

> As if he didn't have anything more productive to give people to do than sweeping the plaza. We went to visit city hall around that time. We had just created a series of women's workshops to make dolls, puppets, and clothes for Christmas. We had about two hundred needy children

in the población then. Everyone in the población contributed something—thread, old clothes—whatever they had.
We explained this project to the local officials. They agreed
to fund about one hundred of these women with money
from the emergency work programs. Later we returned to
request help for the men. Everyone here was unemployed.
Within months we had everyone in the población working—
under our supervision. We got work for the men as carpenters, painters, so that if someone had wood and wanted
another room, or needed something repaired—we sent
the carpenters to help. We held the contracts for all the
workers in the emergency work programs here in this
población. I was the secretary of the governments emergency work programs in Granadilla.

Thus, in 1978, a Communist club, Chile Joven, was
administering emergency employment programs for the
Chilean junta. Political activists in Granadilla always engaged in activities that benefitted the residents of the
población at large.

In 1979, the mayor tried to take control of the población
by demanding that all emergency workers report directly to
him. In so doing he hoped to wrest control of Granadilla's
collective farm, community kitchen and the entire gamut of
popular organizations. The residents of Granadilla responded by unanimously resigning from all government emergency work programs. The community lost access to the
funds that had kept them from starvation. They preferred to
face a precarious future than allow the government to control their población.

Granadilla was also among the few poblaciones able to
provide a real solution for the homeless. Chino observes:

We had over one hundred and fifty homeless families here. We knew that if one hundred and fifty families tried to occupy land waving a Communist flag, we wouldn't be able to remain on the land (not to mention that we'd be shot). So we organized a few families, maybe four or five. City hall closed at five on Friday, so we seized the land at six. By Monday, with the help of the community, we had people living in their homes. When the police arrived they couldn't simply take down a tent but would have to evict entire families with all their belongings, the little they had, from brand new houses.

The houses were made quickly, from a few poles and with the help of the community. The intention was to install the family and everything they owned, so that they could not be sent back. When the police arrived, the families denied involvement in any left-wing political party or organization. "They would say they arrived alone, out of necessity," explains Chino, "but the entire población would then arrive to defend the rights of the families to stay. The political activists would also arrive in the name of solidarity, but in reality it was they who had began the whole process."

Sometimes the police would return at night, with machine guns, firing randomly at the community. The community had to be brave. Eventually, the police stopped coming. Each time the residents occupied a piece of land, they gave five families new homes. Within six months they had a hundred families living in occupied territory. Chino observes:

It didn't make the news, of course, but the families got their houses. You don't have to be that creative, you have to work with the people. When there are many people, ideas flow. Here in the población we discuss everything. The best plans always come from the población—not from the party—from the people themselves. The people here feel proud because of concrete accomplishments. Here there is coherence between our discourse and our actions.

Like other neighborhood organizers, leaders of Granadilla had to develop creative ways of dealing with police repression. The confidence local activists in Granadilla had in their neighbors allowed them considerable success in these endeavors. In 1977, Chino received a call from a secretary at the mayor's office. "Please leave town," she told him. "They are planning to arrest you." He decided to call a town meeting. In the meeting one neighbor suggested they hold a public parade, the next day, to commemorate civil-military relations. They began to organize quickly. They invited the mayor, the press, and the military commanders. All the children lined up, and marched. "Oh they were so happy," recalls Chino. "Then we began the speeches."

First, I spoke. What could I speak about? I couldn't say anything positive about the military, but if I spoke about the Communist Party they would certainly arrest me. So I spoke about the población, about what we, as residents, had accomplished together. The press took photos of me with the military commander. We appeared in all the major papers. It was very difficult to arrest me after that.

Later that year, the local military commander informed the leaders of Chile Joven that the military wanted to hold another celebration on September 11, the anniversary of the coup, to inaugurate Granadilla's collective farm. "Imagine, them inaugurating our farm!" observed Chino. "I told them we still needed many things for the farm—tools, fertilizer, a building to house the community kitchen. Where were we going to hold the inauguration?"

The military sent Chile Joven all that they had requested. Residents worked day and night to build the kitchen. Finally September 11, arrived. The military sent 300 bottles of wine and five hundred meat pies for the celebration. We turned on the ovens at six in the morning. By the time the military arrived, with full regalia, a priest, and a motorcade, the meat pies were ready. "What a wonderful smell," they exclaimed.

"We served them wine and meat pies, but none of us ate anything," laughs Chino. "After the military went home, we still had 250 bottles of wine and 406 meat pies. The next day we had a huge party, full of good wine and meat pies, and we laughed so hard at the joke we had played on the military."

The same year, the residents built a summer camp on the beach of Viña. "We made a collection—money, cloth, and so forth—and built tents. This was the first time the residents of this población had ever seen the beach. It was spectacular. We called it the gypsy camp. For eight days and nights we camped out in our handmade tents with the food we had grown in our communal garden."

Granadilla residents never had a local parish they could turn to for protection. Instead local activists used community solidarity to reclaim the building held by the appointed neighborhood council. The military allowed residents to supply eighteen names to the military commanders for consideration. Six would be selected to run the council. In 1978 nine of those on the community's list were Communists, and the municipality didn't select any of them for office.

The following year, however, the Communists began to organize early. When selection time came, all eighteen of the nominees sent to the municipal government for approval were Communist Party members or sympathizers. The municipality couldn't select any non-Communists. Chino explains that

> that is how we democratized the neighborhood council. It's also how we reconstructed the Communist youth and later the Communist Party. . . . What did we discuss in the party cells? We discussed the población. There wasn't anything else. We discussed the problems of the children, of the youth, of the allegados, and so on. In this type of thing the parties are of no use, because they have no programs or solutions. The party says mobilize, paint, march, but they don't have a plan for the people.

What was significant about the reorganization process in Yungay, Herminda, and Granadilla was the degree to which political activists felt protected by the community. In contrast with Las Parcelas and Lo Hermida, the first organizations created, after the coup, were mass organizations, organizations that included the less political members of the community. It was only in the later stages that the activists began to recreate party cells. This was almost the exact opposite of the process in the less combative poblaciones where activists avoided the mass organizations, fearing informants. In the more combative poblaciones a history of political activity had forged solid grassroots networks that gave political activists more confidence in their neighbors and made political activity under conditions of severe repression feasible. They also helped regenerate the political parties. Putnam argues that networks of civic engagement, like the neighborhood association, choral societies, cooperatives, sports clubs, mass based parties, and the like . . . are an essential form of social capital. The denser such networks in a community the more likely that its citizens will be able to cooperate for mutual benefit (Putnam 1993, 173).

In neighborhoods without a long history of political struggle, however, civic organizations were as likely to support the dictatorship, or to remain neutral, as they were to provide a basis for collective action.

By 1982, there were approximately 1,383 new social organizations in Santiago's poblaciones, with over 200,000 members (Angell 1991, 202), most of whom were women and youth. In 1979, the first citywide poblador organization, the Metropolitana de Pobladores, was formed, with the support of the church. In 1980, the Communists were elected to the presidency of the organization, and a few months later, after a dispute over an illegal land occupation, the Christian Democrats left the Metropolitana and created Solidaridad. In 1982, the MIR created COAPO and the Left Christians created Dignidad. Popular women's groups linked to the political parties also emerged during this period—such as MUDECHI, linked to the Communists, and CODEM, linked to the MIR.

But the small victories of these years were always overshadowed by the one large and looming failure—the persistence of the dictatorship and its economic model. Activists in Yungay, Herminda, and Granadilla, as well as those in other poblaciones, were never free of the shadow of the regime. With time their activities became more openly political, and aggressive. Yet, before 1983 open rebellion would have been impossible.

CHAPTER FIVE

Protests in the Poblaciones

In the first stage of the resistance movement, informal grassroots networks provided the context for political action. In the second stage, a financial crisis, accompanied by national political scandal, gave activists the opportunity to recruit new adherents and mobilize widespread protest. Activists fashioned new broader collective identities, found new selective incentives, and created formal social movement organizations. The return of the traditional political parties overwhelmed informal grassroots networks.

The financial crisis that sparked this new phase of protest activity was a direct consequence of the 1976 deregulation of the banking industry. From 1976 on, financially based clans had taken advantage of negative-interest rate foreign loans, speculating and relending domestically, at rates as high as 18 percent a month. The high-interest loans hamstrung industrial producers, as they struggled to maintain competitiveness against inexpensive imports. By June 1979, growing inflation had made it almost impossible for

153

industry owners to make payments on their loans. Believing that "the rate of price increases in the world economy would automatically regulate domestic inflation," the regime froze the exchange rate (Foxley 1983, 60). The exchange rate in real terms, however, appreciated by almost 30 percent a year, resulting in rapidly expanding trade and current accounts deficits of 10.7 percent and 15.1 percent, respectively, by the end of 1981 (Ffrench-Davis 1983). By 1982, 456 Chilean companies were forced to declare bankruptcy. The total of unpaid debts in the system reached $800 million, while foreign-sector debt rose to $14.8 billion (and continued to rise, reaching $24 billion in 1984). The banking sector alone owed $6.89 billion to foreign institutions. As one businessman complained, "assuming an average interest rate of 30 percent, they should be paying u.s.$3 billion a year out of profits to service the debt. But an open economy such as ours is not capable of generating those profits" (*Latin American Economic Reports* December 1980).

In an attempt to attract new foreign capital, Sergio DeCastro, the Minister of the Economy, freed the exchange rates. Within days, the value of Chilean currency dropped by more than 50 percent. As prices doubled, consumption plummeted, and mass layoffs pushed unemployment figures to 25 percent. Pinochet tried to avert the crisis by giving banking superintendents broad powers to intervene in the affairs of eight banks (Law 18.022). He liquidated two banks and mandated a 5 percent reserve capital for the remaining banks. By May, he was forced to nationalize another ten banks to save them from bankruptcy, and three of the largest remaining were reported to be in trouble. By August industrial production had fallen by 20 percent, bankruptcies had multiplied, and "banks and financial companies exhibited a ratio of bad loans over capital and reserves well in excess of 50 percent, forcing the central bank to intervene, by indirect means, in the whole financial system" (Foxley 1983, 89).

The economic crisis spawned a political crisis. Traditional military supporters, including ex-President Alessandri, and Pablo Rodríguez (head of the neofascist group Fatherland and Liberty), began calling for the creation of a Popular Front to rescue Chile from economic ruin. The conflict between Pinochet and the "Chicago boys" grew so acute that Pinochet dismissed his entire cabinet. (Pinochet would rearrange his cabinet seven times in the next two years. He had changed it six times in the previous nine, making the total number of cabinet changes twice that of any previous government in Chilean history, [*Keesing's Contemporary Archives* 1973–1984].)

The political scandals gave the CTC the courage to prepare a general strike. Decree Law 18,134, which had removed the link between inflation and wage increases, was the catalyst. Mass unemployment, however, made hopes for a prolonged national strike dismal. Fearing that a failed strike would renew the regime's confidence, union leaders searched for a tactic that would maintain pressure on the regime. On May 7, 1983, the unions replaced the general-strike announcement with a call for broad-based protest scheduled for May 11. They asked citizens to show support for the labor movement by turning off lights, boycotting commercial establishments, and symbolically drumming empty pots and pans.

Jack Goldstone argues that "when state strength declines as in a political crisis, the probability of success will go up for all groups . . . [however] the distribution of group protest and success over time would not be uniform, but lumpy, as protest actions and successes cluster around those periods of state vulnerability" (Goldstone 1993, 17). Deteriorating expectations, declining state capacity, and elite cohesion increase the number of groups involved in protest actions. As the number of people involved in protests grow, the risk attached to each action diminishes, since the state must distribute its coercive force against more groups and individuals. Yet, individuals "do not respond only individually . . . they respond as members of distinct communities that mediate between them and the larger structures of economic and political organization" (Sullivan 1992, 232).

In Chile, the 1983 economic crisis acted as a signaling event. The crisis led many to arrive at similar assessments of declining state capacity, and in so doing, triggered widespread protest action. Protest did not spread equally, however, throughout Santiago. The neighborhoods that were most active during the 1983–1986 protest cycle were those most closely linked, historically, to the Chilean Communist Party. In these neighborhoods strong grassroots networks allowed protesters to take advantage of declining state capacity.

Thus, while the 1982 economic crisis had its most devastating impact in the western zone of Santiago (in the suburbs of Pudahuel and Quilicura) where monthly average incomes dropped from 32,000 pesos in 1980 to 16,000 in 1983 (data provided to author by the Departamento de Economía de Universidad de Chile in 1986), protest activity was comparatively light in most of the shantytowns in this district. In the first protests, residents did little more than build barricades and drum pots and pans. Only in a few poblaciones did residents even organize marches (Centro de Estudios de Trabajo 1983, hereafter referred to as CETRA/ CEAL, 13–16). The division between activists and residents allowed the military to arrest, or disappear, the most active members of the community and silence the rest.

Comparatively, the 1982 economic crisis hardly affected Santiago's southern zone. Between 1980 and 1983, monthly incomes dropped from thirty-six thousand to twenty-six thousand in San Miguel and from twenty-three thousand to seventeen thousand in La Granja (data provided to author by the Departamento de Economía de Universidad de Chile in 1986). Yet, from the beginning, the southern zone residents fought hardest and most violently against the dictatorship. In traditional Communist poblaciones, such as La Victoria and Yungay, residents engaged in an avalanche of popular rebellion. They built burning barricades made from branches, tires and garbage, and turned the streets into a battle ground between military forces and stone throwing pobladores (CETRA/CEAL 1983; *Hechos Urbanos* 1983, No. 23 Suplemento; Rodríguez 1983). Strong grassroots networks, trust between neighbors, and a history of successful collective action imbued residents with the courage and confidence to confront the regime. As Ana recalls, the first protest in Yungay began when residents gathered to defend activists from police repression:

> The human rights committee, of which I was president, and the Christian-base community had organized a hunger strike, a nonviolent act. Yet when the police arrived, they began to arrest everyone, including the priest. Residents of the población came to defend us. They began to throw rocks at the police. The police arrested several residents, but fled the población quickly. That evening the

residents built barricades and set them on fire. Burning barricades lit every corner of the población.

Irma, a Christian Democrat, says that communal solidarity made the first protests in Yungay feel like a carnival. "The first tire brought to the barricades came with the whole población behind it. We weren't afraid. They could kill us, but they would kill us fighting for our rights. Here when they tried to arrest people, the whole población would jump to their defense."

On the day of the first national protest, two pobladores were killed, fifty injured and three hundred were detained (CETRA/CEAL 1983). The worst repression, however, was reserved for the traditional communist neighborhoods. Ana remembers vividly the repression in Yungay:

> Several days after the first protest the police arrived with tanks, helicopters and armed soldiers. They arrested all the men and held them in Brazil Park. The secret police arrived next. They destroyed entire houses and terrorized families. We tried to find out what was happening to the men. We began to burn newspapers, pamphlets, and documents. Then they began to release the men, but they did not release my husband, Bernardo, until five in the afternoon. They were torturing him, publicly, in front of the hundreds of prisoners held in Brazil Park.

The severity of the repression made it difficult for the residents of poblaciones lacking such strong networks to maintain resistance. In these poblaciones, the apparent weakness of the regime, combined with the call for protest by a moderate labor movement, had convinced residents that the protests might be successful. When residents were forced to confront the regime's repressive apparatus without organizational support, however, they quickly retreated. Leo criticizes the incapacity of the political activists to lead the protests in Las Parcelas:

> The first protests were very exciting. There were so many people suddenly in the streets. Many had come because of our agitation and propaganda. We taught them to build barricades and to dig trenches so the police could not enter the población. But we did not know what else to do with them. We were unable to take advantage of their eagerness to act. We did not know how to say "let's get organized, let's take advantage of every opportunity." The people went into the streets and were beaten. They did not know how to defend themselves, why they were there, or where they were going.

Similarly, a member of a cultural group in Villa O'Higgens observes, "there were many protests here in 1983, but they were mostly spontaneous. We were unable to maintain them or defend the community." A local organizer in Lo Hermida notes, the organizations created during the flood were not prepared to address problems beyond the immediate crisis. The soup kitchens, in particular

> play a terrible role—only managing hunger. They are very antiparty, they fear being used by the parties, and, as a result, lack political direction. This is really a failure of the political parties . . . the inability to move beyond the immediate problems of the soup kitchens and create mass organizations with clear political projects. The community lacks good leaders with a clear sense of what must be done.

In Yungay, La Victoria, and Herminda de la Victoria, by contrast, even severe repression could not deter residents from staging further demonstrations against the regime. Instead, residents learned to organize better and to develop new methods of self-defense. Violeta, of Herminda de la Victoria, recalls:

> We learned to defend ourselves, much as a child learns to walk, little by little. We discovered who was who, who opened doors for one to hide. As the repression grew more severe, we learned new strategies of defense. We began to create new organizations, marching from población to población, by foot, organizing.

During the month following the first protest members of the Comando Nacional de Trabajadores (CNT, National Workers Union) forged a *comando* for the second protest. Concurrently, women's groups organized marches and sit-ins in front of the Cathedral to protest the dictatorship and commemorate those killed during the coup. The number of popular economic organizations in Santiago increased from 494 in November 1982 to 702 by March 1984 (Valdes 1987, 43).

On June 11, 1983, Santiago again exploded in protest. Thousands of Chileans flooded the streets of Santiago, pounding their pots and pans and demanding an immediate return to democratic rule. Children stayed home from school, and factories and commercial establishments closed early. University students sprayed walls with political slogans, occupied campuses, and built flaming barricades in the heart of the city. Drivers honked their horns in the streets while pedestrians marched through the streets beating empty pots and pans. Commercial establishments and factories closed early or failed to open at all. In the poblaciones residents held hunger strikes or attacked symbols of local authority such as minimum employment offices and fire stations and looted local supermarkets, distributing food to residents. The strongest protests were still in Santiago's southern zone where young residents fought armed soldiers and tanks with stones and makeshift weapons. Now, however, the protests in several poblaciones in the western zone, such as Herminda de la Victoria and Violeta Parra grew increasingly violent (CETRA/CEAL 1983; *Hechos Urbanos* 1983; Rodríguez 1983). When the armed forces attacked these poblaciones, residents responded by pelting the tanks with rocks. By dawn clouds of tear gas floated over the poblaciones. Violeta remembers:

> We had set up a little club in the football field, with a gate and light. On the day of the first national protest, goodbye field, goodbye gate, goodbye light. More protests, more broken light bulbs, more trees torn down, more barricades, more repression, more tear gas. It was as if everyone in the población had this rage. Residents ran to their homes and grabbed whatever they could put their hands on and pah, it was immediately in the street. No one examined what it was they had, they just threw it into the street. The barricades grew higher than seemed possible. Suddenly no one was afraid, no one feared for their life. It all happened so quickly.

The surge of protest activity catapulted the political parties back into the public arena, giving protesters access to a much larger array of resources and national communication networks. The Christian Democratic Party soon assumed formal leadership of the movement, astutely taking advantage or the new political space opened by the protests.

They enjoyed clear advantages over the parties of the Left:

> Its principal leaders and public figures had remain[ed] in Chile and [were] often quoted in the press. Its labor and student leaders [were] public figures. The party retain[ed] certain media channels, including the country's largest weekly news magazine, a radio station, and publishing houses. . . . The relative ease with which the party has been able to act in Chile allowed it to renew its top leadership, to hold frequent meetings with current and past middle and even local leaders, and to hold consultation for informative purposes with a significant portion of the rank and file (Valenzuela and Valenzuela 1986a, 141).

The regime's weakness also led to increasing political coordination between groups. "While strong ties within groups may be crucial to action by specific groups, weak ties across groups are equally vital if action is to become more than local action for specific goals, and coalesce into effective revolutionary action" (Goldstone 1993, 21). In July political activists forged new local protest comandos. The local comandos, in turn, united to form the Coordinadoras de Organizaciones Sociales Populares (Coalition of Popular Organizations). At the national level, fifty-four political leaders signed a document demanding the immediate resignation of Pinochet. The bishops also issued a declaration of protest.

Simultaneously, copper miners, truckers, and university students stepped up organizing activity, launching major strikes throughout the country. The government responded by militarizing the mines, firing the striking miners, and imposing a midnight curfew. It also attacked Christian Democratic leaders, arresting Gabriel Valdés (president of the

DC), Rodolfo Seguel (head of the CNT), and other leaders of the CNT.

In July, the political parties called for a third national protest day, on the eleventh. This time the mobilizations spread throughout Chile, imbuing Chileans with new confidence in the possibility of political change. The cultural symbols of the movement mobilized the less traditionally active public, but even in smaller cities like Valparaiso, the traditional Communist shantytowns were the most active. Chino, for instance, remembers, massive protests in Granadilla:

> Children, women, everyone participated. Everyone here knew everyone else. If a strange vehicle arrived, everyone knew immediately. Battles raged from morning until midnight. Everyone cooperated, whether they belonged to a political party, or not. We put "caps" in the streets so that when the police arrived, they would set off a loud noise. The police were afraid, because they though it might be a bomb. But they returned, angrier and better prepared. When they attacked us, they used real bullets. So many were wounded. We began to organize militarily, but without arms. Like Indians, we organized silently, in the dark— so that the police could not enter the población.

Pobladores and university students now led the movement. In Santiago young people set fire to local government offices such as POJH, Centros de Madres CEMA, women's centers (called mothers' centers), and Chilectra (public utilities). In some poblaciones young people threw stones at electric cables, causing electric power failures. The first armed actions also occurred during this protest, directed against electric towers. At the end of the third national protest day, two protesters were dead and over a thousand arrested (De la Maza and Garcés 1985, 54).

In the month following the July protest, students reclaimed student centers. Student organizations and women's groups forged a new national women's federation called Movimiento pro Emancipación de la Mujer (MEMCH). The most important organization to emerge during this period was the Alianza Democrática (AD, Democratic Alliance) formed by the Christian Democrats, the Altamirano wing of the Socialist Party, the Radical Party, the MAPU, and other small parties. The Altamirano Socialists, the far left during the Unidad Popular, by this time had come to believe that the failure of the Unidad Popular was due to its inability to win the support of the middle classes and political center. At the core of its new coalitional strategy was the Alianza Democrática.

Pobladores in the eastern zone of Santiago also became active during this period (CETRA/CEAL 1983; *Hechos Urbanos* 1983, No. 23 Suplemento; Rodríguez 1983). By the end of July, a major confrontation between pobladores and police erupted in the población Lo Hermida. The government increased repression against local parishes, but it also attempted to appease the more moderate opposition leaders. It replaced several cabinet members, released Seguel and Valdés, and gave a new group of exiles authorization to return.

By August, the tacit alliance between the left and center opposition had begun to thin. The Alianza Democrática, with the CNT, called for a fourth day of national protest (choosing the eleventh so that the fifth national protest would coincide with the tenth year anniversary of the coup), with the intention of forcing the regime to respond to its demands. In the poblaciones, however, local leftist activists were already organizing for a two-day protest, and had begun to train residents in self-defense, in preparation for an eventual insurrection.

Pinochet took advantage of the growing schism. He savagely attacked shantytowns residents and the political left while initiating a dialogue with leaders of the center-right. He reorganized his cabinet, abandoning the Chicago model. On August 11, Pinochet ordered eighteen thousand troops into the streets in response to the fourth national day of demonstrations. One hundred twenty-nine protesters were shot, twenty-nine fatally. Over a thousand protesters were detained, and subjected to torture.

In the week following the August massacre, Pinochet announced a political opening. A dialogue with the Alianza Democrática would be initiated, on the government's behalf, by Sergio Onafre Jarpa, the new, and first civilian, minister of interior. The government lifted the state of emergency, legalized non-Marxist parties and allowed a large group of exiles to return. The Alianza Democrática agreed to suspend the protests, if the government provide a calendar of transition and promise to investigate the human rights abuses documented by the Vicaría.

The illegal parties of the Left, the MIR, the Communists, and the remaining sectors of the Socialists, called a press conference—marking their first public appearance. Pobladores in the southern zone of Santiago staged a long march, despite severe military repression. Teachers and other professionals held marches as well.

In September, the Alianza Democrática called for a single day of protest on the eighth of September. The illegal leftist parties called for four days of protest, beginning on the eighth and lasting until the eleventh. The protests began, then, with all of the political parties participating. Activists staged six separate acts in memory of Salvador Allende, while students held marches and demonstrations in universities and high schools. In the center of town, protesters held a nonviolent sit-in. In the copper mines, workers led hunger strikes, and in the poblaciones, protesters engaged in pitched battles with armed police. The next day struggles in the poblaciones grew even more violent. By the tenth of September, funeral marches for the dead had become the scene of new battles between the police and the poor. All told, four days of protest left fifteen dead, four hundred injured, and six hundred in detention.

The illegal parties of the Left now formed their own political coalition called the Movimiento Democrático Popular (MDP, Democratic Popular Movement). While the Alianza Democrática had viewed the protests as a means of forcing the government to negotiate, the MDP rejected dialogue and called for all forms of struggle, including violence, in the battle against the dictatorship.

This new strategy reflected the dramatic changes undergone by both the Communist Party and Almeyda wing of the Socialist Party. Until 1979 the Communist Party had put a marked emphasis on the political means of democratizing the country. The severity of the repression, however, provoked serious debate. Some members of the central committee in exile accused the Party of being naive and argued that it was time for the Party to develop a military strategy. (Cademártori interview with author March 1988, New York). In late 1978 Gladys Marín, General Secretary of the Communist Youth, returned from Cuba with a small group of Communist exiles. Along with other members of the underground in Chile, they constructed a clandestine Equipo de Dirección and an armed apparatus fashioned after the Frente Sandinista. By 1980 the party had given up hope of an alliance with the Christian Democratic Party. The only method left with which to deal with the extreme military repression was to prepare a military offensive. The success of the Nicaraguan revolution in 1979 reinforced their resolve. The change in orientation of the leaders of the U.S.S.R also profoundly affected Chilean Party leaders living in Moscow. At the twenty-sixth congress Leonid Brezhnev insisted that "regimes must know how to defend themselves." (Communists in El Salvador also adopted the slogan "all forms of struggle are valid" shortly after the conference.)

The Almeyda Socialists (the moderates during the Unidad Popular) went through a similar conversion. If the Altamirano Socialists (the radicals during the Unidad Popular) had come to believe that a coalition with the Christian Democrats was the key to success, the Almeyda Socialists had come to believe that the failure of the Unidad Popular was caused by "the lack of a revolutionary vanguard . . . and the incorrect assumption that it was possible to carry out the revolutionary process within bourgeois institutions" (Furci 1984, 144). On this basis, the Party

> suggested the type of party necessary in Chile's present political circumstances: an organization based on Leninist democratic centralism, purged of the petty bourgeois revolutionaries, homogeneous in its program and ideology—a party that must constitute the disciplined and homogeneous revolutionary vanguard of the masses, with its very strict unity in its rank and file" (Furci 1984, 144).

The Almeyda Socialists, thus, found themselves, again, very close to the Communist Party. The Altamirano and Almeyda Socialists reunited during this period into the Bloque Socialista (Socialist Bloc), but while the Altamirano wing remained in the Alianza Democrática, the Almeyda wing joined the Communist Party and the MIR in the MDP.

In September, the Alianza Democrática began yet a third round of dialogue with the government and refused to participate in any more protests. As one Christian Democratic activist confided, "the protests are like a party crashed by people who were not invited." Excluded from the talks, the MDP now assumed leadership of the movement and called for a sixth national three-day protest, from the eleventh until the thirteenth of October. The Christian Democratic Youth, far to the left of its parent party, rejected the lead of the older DC and announced support for all forms of protest. The refusal of the Alianza Democrática, however, to endorse this call severely hampered the mass mobilizations. Isolated, the residents of shantytowns were now defenseless against military repression. Only in Communist poblaciones, were activists able to mobilize protest. As a young organizer in Pablo Neruda, a section of La Pincoya observed in 1986, community support in these poblaciones lessened the level of risk attached to protest actions: "The solidarity here is very great, and that helps the community defend itself. Everyone here opens their doors to protesters escaping the military or police." Similarly, Carlos, interviewed in Joao Goulart in 1989, noted the contrast between organizing protests in Joao Goulart and organizing in Yungay: "In my población I was always afraid that someone would denounce me. Yungay was different. In Yungay the level of support was incredible, and reduced our risk."

Altogether five pobladores were killed in the September protest.

By the end of September, the CNT, frustrated with the slow pace of reform, lead the call for protests on the twenty-seventh of October. This time both the MDP and the AD supported the call. On October 27, the seventh national protest day, protests again erupted throughout Santiago. By the end of the day, thirty demonstrators were injured (sixteen with bullet wounds) and one hundred were arrested.

Between November 1983 and March 1984, there were no more calls for national protest. Political activity, however, did not entirely cease. In the more politicized poblaciones, activists focused their efforts on rebuilding social organizations, strengthening community ties, and reviving cultural traditions. Often they created alternate forms of grassroots democracy. In Yungay, for instance, residents held block meetings and elected a representative on each block. The block representatives chose twelve delegates to form the new democratic neighborhood council. The president of the neighborhood council explains:

> Everyone in the población participated in the selection. We challenged the legitimacy of the government's neighborhood council and embarked on a plan of action. As we began to produce ideas, we awakened the población. We began a momentum, a rhythm. First we created a building and demanded a telephone from the municipality. We told the municipality that we would take them to court if they did not give us a telephone. To avoid a suit, they must come with us to the notary and sign the papers giving us the rights to a telephone. They accepted. We made a public declaration and a contract requiring them to install

a telephone in our building. We now have a telephone, which is open to the community from 8:00 A.M. to midnight.

The democratic neighborhood council, then, used the money collected from telephone calls to buy the community an ambulance (they charged 20 pesos a call, the normal price for a telephone call in Chile). "The neighbors began to have more confidence in us," the president of the neighborhood council observed. "They became more involved in the process. They worked more. With unity and democracy, all of the sectors in the población got involved."

Next, the neighborhood council opened a library, the first library in the area. They called it Pablo Neruda Library, after the famous Communist poet. "All of this was done on our own," the president proudly acknowledges:

> We received no help from anyone outside the población, neither economic nor material. Next we began to create sidewalks. We never had sidewalks. We constructed five thousand meters of sidewalks. The neighbors laid the cement. The municipality provided the materials. They say they gave them to us, but in reality they robbed us. They bought the materials with the money they took from the community. They have to provide these things.

With each successful struggle the residents grew bolder, they developed more confidence in themselves and a broader conception of their rights as citizens. The president of the democratic neighborhood council in 1986 observed:

> We told the mayor, we bought this población. We began the construction and the military robbed us. The munici-

pality has been an accomplice in this. We paid for fully urbanized housing and we were not provided with it.

We used to think that we had to give something to receive something from the municipality. Now we demand that which we deserve, what accrues to us as citizens of this country. We demand what is legally ours. We demand our rights.

Community solidarity enabled the neighborhood council to challenge the legitimacy of the government's appointed representatives. It allowed the community to reassert its democratic will. The president of the neighborhood council explains:

> When we demand these things, the other neighborhood council does not say anything, for fear that the mayor will simply dismiss them. We, on the other hand, have the población on our side. He can not fire us, he did not hire us. When he tries to throw us out, the entire población says NO. Unity rises from democratic foundations. There was always a great deal of solidarity in our población and a great desire to fight against the regime. We suffered a great deal. Never, however, did we have the level of participation we have now. Now we have more comprehension, more unity, more solidarity.

Sometimes the neighborhood council used the law to apply pressure, but usually they relied on the people themselves, the community, to apply pressure. Every week they called a meeting in every sector. "We are always in meetings," insisted the president of the council, adding, "We work through grassroots democracy. The people support the neighborhood council with their own funds. Everyone contributes something even when they do not have enough to eat," a member of the high-school support group told me. "The mayor has created his own neighborhood council, with all the government money, but we ignore it."

This stress on participation and collective identity helped activists rebuild the community's confidence. As an organizer in Pablo Neruda, explains:

> Cultivating a collective identity is an essential element in the struggle. We try to preserve in our community a sense of dignity, pride and identification as pobladores. Every year we celebrate the anniversary of the land occupation of our población. We try to raise the communities consciousness—We took this land, it was not given.

In Yungay, where the población was not born from an illegal land seizure, activists encouraged residents to identify with working-class struggles fought before anyone in the población was even born. As one Yungay resident proudly announced:

> Here we have a history of combativeness, dating from the struggles in the nitrate mines at the turn of the century. Here we have the capacity to organize and resist. They can repress and kill us as individuals, but the organizations survive and the resistance rises again.

In November 1983, the Alianza Democrática held a legal rally in O'Higgens park. Half a million people attended. Although organized by the Christian Democrats, the rally attested to the public revival of the Left. Communist, Socialist, and Mirista flags waved throughout the park.

Just when the Communist Party discovered new forms of legal and institutional resistance, it launched its first act of armed resistance. On December 14, 1983, the Frente Patriótico Manuel Rodríguez, the new guerilla wing of the Communist Party, took over a radio station in Santiago, and dedicated itself to the armed defence of the people. Within the next few months the Frente launched a series of attacks on electric power plants. The government responded with increasing repression against the PC and the MIR. In March the military took two suspected Miristas, tied them with several sticks of dynamite and blew them up. The military also raided the poblaciones and arrested hundreds of residents. The dialogue between the Christian Democrats and the government stopped.

In March 1984, the Alianza Democrática returned to the opposition, joining the CNT in the call for an eighth national protest day, for March 27. The major union, professional, and small business organizations backed the call with significant consequences. "The enormity of the protests, the early closing of commercial establishments, the cessation of public transportation, and the severity of the repression (including an 8:30 P.M. curfew), meant that by the afternoon of the twenty-seventh, all activities in the capital city were virtually at a stand still" (De la Maza and Garcés 1985, 54). Pobladores looted supermarkets, set buses aflame, and severed electric cables, causing blackouts through much of the city. Confrontations between stone throwing residents and armed military and police occurred in several more mobilized neighborhoods. The Frente stepped up its attacks, blowing up one train station and bombing several buses and utility plants. By the end of the day, 7 protesters were dead, 63 wounded, and 638 under arrest.

Throughout April, workers, students, and pobladores

continued to engage in strikes, hunger strikes, marches, demonstrations, and confrontations with police. On May Day a peaceful rally in O'Higgens Park was attended by 2,500 people. Simultaneously, armed actions against power stations, supermarkets, newspapers, and television stations, police buses, and military barracks escalated. Political repression continued to climb, and 247 activists were arrested. By the end of the month the Alianza Democrática, with the support of the church, had forged a new coalition called the National Accord for the Return to Democracy (Acuerdo Nacional). It included all the political parties except the Communists and the MIR. The leaders of the Acuerdo Nacional argued that the protests had become too costly, and that the opposition must initiate a new dialogue with the government. The Communist Party, which espoused violence, was to be excluded from both the coalition and the dialogue.

Isolated, the MDP announced that it would continue the mobilizations and strikes until the regime fell, a forecast that, given the circumstances, appeared unlikely to all but the most devoted members of the Left. While the parties of Acuerdo Nacional endorsed the May protests as a symbolic display to force the regime to negotiate, the parties of the MDP had begun to see the protests as the first step toward a prolonged national strike and a revolutionary insurrection. In this light, the May 11, 1984, protest, held on the anniversary of the first protest, was an abysmal failure. The level of political mobilization abated, but the repression did not. By the end of the first day, one protester was dead, twenty-two wounded, and one hundred seventy under arrest.

Between May and September, both opposition coalitions reevaluated their strategies. The Christian Democrats decided to further distance themselves from the Left, to solicit the support of the right-wing Nationalist Party, and to reinspire the middle classes, which had grown disillusioned with the protests. Pinochet took advantage of the MDP's growing isolation to pass new antiterrorist legislation and escalate attacks against suspected members of armed groups. The success of any national protest depended on the level of protest activity in those poblaciones with weak grassroots networks. Since they were only mobilized when a strong national coalition led the call for protests, the split between the Alianza Democrática and the MDP drastically reduced the size of the demonstrations. Human-rights abuses also proliferated during this period, and eight left-wing activists were assassinated in alleged confrontations with police. The regime also pushed legislation to censor the left-wing press.

Many grassroots activists began to shift strategy, some focusing on democratizing neighborhood councils and organizing around community needs, while others began to move into clandestine military organizations. As one young activist, interviewed in 1989 recalls: "We were not getting anywhere. I wanted to fight the regime directly, so I joined the Frente." Other activists, however, took the opposite view. As one activist, in 1986, argued:

> It is difficult to ask people to continue risking death when they are not gaining any ground by their efforts. We have to develop new forms of protest to regenerate falling confidence in the movement, but we must always focus on the community's immediate necessities. Vanguard parties do not work. Success is more likely when we fight for solutions to problems close at home.

In June, university students and pobladores, organized mostly by the Left, engaged in a variety of protest events. These included hunger strikes in the El Teniente copper mine, a general strike in the poblaciones in the western zone of Santiago (Pudahuel), a protest march by eighty journalists in Valparaiso, hunger marches in Santiago and Concepción, electric blackouts in several provinces, and thirty-one bombing incidents in ten cities. Poblador organizations launched several illegal land occupations during this period. In July, for instance, eight thousand families participated in a toma that led to the creation of campamentos Monseñor Fresno and Silva Henríquez. As one participant recalls:

> The repression was so severe that the occupants were forced to separate and occupy two plots of land. Since there were not enough political leaders to direct two new settlements, most of activists grouped in Silva Henríquez, leaving the Campamento Fresno vulnerable to infiltration by the most reactionary forces. Less than a year later, the military invaded Silva Henríquez and arrested the members of the neighborhood council, along with the other local political leaders. Over one hundred were exiled to a concentration camp in the northern desert town of Pisagua.

Of the twenty-four land occupations attempted by poblador organizations between 1980 and 1985, this one was the only successful one, even if its success was extremely limited.

The Christian Democrats criticized the growing violence and lawlessness of the Left opposition and called for a Journey for Life, for August 9, with the Catholic Church, as protest against both protest violence and the regime's escalating human-rights abuse. Diverse middle-class organiza-

CATHY LISA SCHNEIDER

A young resident of Campamento Fresno, 1986.

tions, Christian-based communities, and Christian Democratic leaders held a nonviolent demonstration in front of the cathedral. "Gracias a la Vida" was sung in diverse sectors of Santiago. The regime arrested thirty-four protesters during the one-day Journey for Life. Ten young pobladores were killed in confrontations with police the next day and another forty-five were arrested. The regime threatened the opposition with a massacre equivalent to that of September 11, 1973 (De la Maza and Garcés 1985, 60–64).

By the end of August, it was clear to the Christian Democrats that their fourth attempt at a negotiated transition had failed. The Nationalist Party refused to join the opposition; the regime had refused to offer concessions; and the Journey for Life had left ten dead and human-rights abuses on the rise. Frustrated, the DC joined the MDP in calling for a new wave of protest activity. "Only through protest," it asserted, "can we advance along the path of dialogue" (De la Maza and Garcés 1985, 62).

The Alianza Democrática convoked the tenth national protest under the banner, "without protest there is no change." For the first time, the protests were explicitly designed to paralyze the city—as the backbone of a national strike. The streets became the main arena of activity, barricades and *miguelitos* (nails designed to puncture tires) became the most important form of protest. Young pobladores emerged as the protests central protagonists. Young people constructed burning barricades on main thoroughfares to block transit, and in so doing, prevented commercial activity throughout the city.

By the afternoon of September 4, the protests had paralyzed the city. Commercial establishments and public buses retired early. Schools had less than 50 percent attendance. Students, shantytown dwellers, workers, and professionals marched through the streets of Santiago banging empty pots and pans. Violent confrontations between students and police erupted at the Pedagógico, the Medical College, and engineering departments of the University of Chile and at the Universidad de Santiago. Student protesters seized the president's office at the Pedagógico.

The government tried to quell the demonstrations with dogs, water canons, tear gas, tanks, bullets, and even bombs directed against university students and pobladores. In the población La Victoria the priest Andrés Jarlan was shot to death. Three other protesters were killed on September 4, three more were wounded, and 340 were arrested. The following day the protests spread to Copiapó, in the North, and Concepción, in the South. At the Universidad de Atacama, in Copiapo, 400 students were arrested, and 15 injured. At the Universidad de Concepción, 100 students were arrested, 25 injured. By the end of the 2nd day of protest 10 were dead, over 50 wounded, and over a thousand under arrest. After the general strikes of September, the movement had new momentum. The Federación de Estudiantes de Universidad de Chile (FECH, Student Federation of the University of Chile), and Federación de Estudiantes de Universidad Católica (FEUC, Student Federation of Catholic University) reemerged. In the shantytowns, activists created new organizations, and, by January 1985, two hundred thousand pobladores were participating in base-level organizations (Valdes 1987, 43). The three leading leftist shantytown organizations (The Communist, Metro, the Mirista, COAPO; and the Left Christian, Dignidad) began attempts at creating a single coordinating body. The Church, on the other hand, called for moderation, while it acknowledged the right of dissent (De la Maza and Garcés 1985, 67). Military repression grew more intense, in particular against journalists and other members of the opposition media. A church in Punta Arenas was bombed, and a young poblador disappeared, his tortured body found several weeks later.

It was in this context of increasing political violence that the CNT, with the support of the MDP, launched the tenth national protest. Alianza Democrática leaders expressed solidarity with movement coordinators. Although the Alianza did not participate directly, its expression of support gave the protesters a renewed sense of unity and confidence.

On October 29, the protests began in preparation for the general strike to be held the following day. Early in the morning, in support of the strike, pobladores began to build the *fogatas* (burning barricades) and set the miguelitos. Again, the strongest protests were in La Victoria, La Legua, Yungay, Herminda de la Victoria, and Violeta Parra. Yet, now the less organized poblaciones like Sara Gajardo, Lo Hermida, Villa O'Higgens, and Las Parcelas also mobilized. In the center of town women, journalists, and labor unionists held rallies and marches. On October 30, self-defense militias mobilized in the poblaciones and protests grew increasingly violent. Young people threw stones at buses and commercial establishments that refused to strike. Absenteeism, in both schools and work, reached 70 and 46 percent, respectively (De la Maza and Garcés 1985, 70). Transportation ground to a standstill with only 10 percent running by midday (De la Maza and Garcés 1985, 71). Commercial establishments partly shut in the morning were completely shut down by 4:00 P.M. Assaults on electric power stations blacked out much of the country.

Pinochet responded with threats and assaults. The military raided hundreds of shantytowns, arresting close to a thousand pobladores. Two hundred and sixty-five were exiled to the concentration camp Pisagua in the northern desert. Pinochet declared that he would not negotiate, would not alter the constitution or its time table for transition, but would instead order a three-month state of siege.

In March 1985, the carabineros kidnaped three militants of the Communist Party. Their bodies were left in a ditch in the distant población of Quilicura. They had been tortured, their throats had been cut, and they had been left to slowly bleed to death. The government renewed the state of siege for another three months.

In April 1985, the United States Congress, for the first time since 1980, pressured the Reagan administration to abstain on a series of IMF and World Bank loans. While the loans passed, in June, U.S. officials insisted that they could not guarantee the passage of any more loans until Pinochet lifted the state of siege; which he did in July 1985.

By August of 1985, protests were again underway. Weekly protests, which had begun in March to demand justice for the murdered Communists (called, in Chile, the *degollados*—the butchered), escalated. Hundreds of Chileans marched in front of the palace of justice every Friday at 1:00 P.M. At the end of August, the government admitted that the carabineros had assassinated the three Communist leaders. General Mendoza, head of the carabineros, became the second general forced to leave the junta. Other carabineros who had been charged with the assassinations were also arrested but were released a few weeks later.

On September 4, 1985, the unions called for a protest in commemoration of the last democratic election. The military responded to the new wave of protests with tanks and bullets. Hundreds of demonstrators were wounded, ten fatally, including three children under five who were shot when bullets penetrated the paper thin walls of their homes.

In November 1985, the Alianza Democrática held a legal, authorized, public assembly in O'Higgens Park. Over half a million people attended, including militants from the excluded Communist Party and MIR. In December 1985 Pinochet rejected yet another proposal, initiated by the Acuerdo Nacional. In January 1986, the leaders of Chile's popular and professional organizations organized a new coalition, the Asamblea de Civilidad (Civic Assembly), which, for the first time, included representatives of both the Communist Party and the MIR. Unlike the Acuerdo Nacional, the leaders of the new Asamblea de Civilidad centered their strategy on frequent and intense social mobilizations, designed to make the country ungovernable.

The mobilizations began in the universities in March. Medical and professional associations took up the banner in April. On May 20, 1986, the unions called for a massive procession down the Alameda, the main street of Santiago. The military responded to the unions' announcement by cordoning off the city, forbidding anyone to enter or leave. By 5:00 P.M., thousands of commuters jammed the bridges and throughways. Near the law school at the University of Chile, students, unable to cross the bridges over the river Mapuche, began a series of dances and protest chants. The military tolerated the demonstrations for nearly an hour. Suddenly, at dusk, they opened fire on the dancing university students. As the students fled in terror, a nineteen-year-old medical student, Ronald Woods, was shot dead— increasing the total of civilian protest deaths to two hundred (Lozza 1986, 22).

The culmination of the Asamblea strategy was the general strike of July 2–3 1986. As a young activist in the poorly organized shantytown Villa O'Higgens noted during a September 1986 interview, even in the least organized shantytowns protesters felt new confidence:

In 1986, confidence increased because of the organization of the political parties and the clarity of their new strategy. The July 2–3 general strike was especially strong

The cover of the July 1986 Que Hacemos *showing Verónica
DeNegri (bottom center) marching at the funeral of her son,
Rodrigo Rojas DeNegri. The author is directly behind
Verónica DeNegri.*

because of a comando unit for the general strike made up of leaders of all political parties within the población. The organization and publicity began early, and there was support from many other sectors—such as the mobilization of doctors and other professionals.

Similarly, the priest in Sara Gajardo, another less organized población on the border of Herminda de la Victoria, observed, during an interview in October 1986:

> In the strike of July 2 and 3, 1986, participation reached a peak here. A good campaign of diffusion and propaganda, and a good organizing effort, was the main reason. Organizers spoke with parents, shop owners, bus drivers, trade unions. The convocation was wider—included the middle sectors and the trade unions. They created the conditions for something both massive and simultaneous. The slogan of the assembly was everyone together simultaneously. The national strikes of March 1984 and October 1985 were also very successful for similar reasons. If there is a large massive movement, and all the political parties work together, we can close-off Sara Gajardo to the repressive forces. If we cannot close off the población, we move all our resources to Salvador Gutiérrez, the main artery of Herminda de la Victoria.

The day before the protest, the wife, sister, and daughter of a folk singer were murdered in their home in another shantytown. That evening, flaming barricades blocked traffic throughout the city. Protests the following day paralyzed the city. Eighty-five percent of factories and commercial establishments ceased operations (Monckeberg and Juanita-

CATHY LISA SCHNEIDER

Padre Aldunate blessing the mural commemorating the two young people, Carmen Gloria Quintana and Rodrigo Rojas De Negri, set afire while still alive, on July 2, 1986.

rojas 1986, 10–14). The government reacted to the mobilizations with a new wave of political violence. In Los Nogales, the military grabbed two young people, aged seventeen and eighteen (Carmen Gloria Quintana and Rodrigo Rojas), beat them, doused them with gasoline and set them on fire (the boy died four days later, the girl survived, massively scarred). A thirteen-year-old girl was shot and killed on her way to buy bread, one of six who were shot to death. Fifty were shot and wounded. More than six hundred were arrested in the two days of protest, most of them severely beaten or tortured.

In August, a visit from United States General John Galvin coincided with Pinochet's announcement of the discovery of arsenals hidden in the North. The Communist Party had been secretly stockpiling weapons. The discovery of the arsenals triggered shock waves throughout the country. The Christian Democrats denounced the Communists for their use of violence and rejected the call for a general strike for the fourth of September. Still, the Communists refused to call off the strike. The MIR argued that a two-day strike was too short, and that the strike would be indefinitely prolonged. The confusion surrounding the strike plans and the divisions among the opposition parties frightened both the middle class and the poor. Protesters were active only in the traditional Communist poblaciones. Without outside support, however, the residents of these communities suffered the entire weight of military casualties.

On September 4, the military occupied the poblaciones in anticipation of the general strike. Armed soldiers patrolled the streets, making it impossible to cross from one house to the next without help from neighborhood sentries. In a home in Villa O'Higgens, a five-year-old boy greeted me with a toy gun. "This is to stop the soldiers from breaking in," he told me. Yet there were no protests there on the fourth of September. The high rate of fatalities on the second and third of July and the confusion surrounding the strike plans for September convinced the vast majority that the risk was simply too great. As one local human-rights advocate observed:

> The problem is lack of clarity, the failure of the parties to agree and have a clear project; the refusal of the Christian

Democrats to be involved in the strike; the failure of the professionals to participate in any actions; the lack of any kind of mobilization two months prior; the lack of publicity; the lack of confidence; the disappointment after the high level of injuries in the July strike which, here in Villa O'Higgens, included fourteen bullet injuries, five injuries from bird shot, thirty-four arrests, and one death.

There is much repression here, because this community is important, strategically, yet there is little organization here to defend it.

As we were talking, the military arrived and began shooting at the homes and church, although no protests were taking place. The shooting continued without interruption for four hours.

"The repression began to destroy the movement," Leo cogently observed, years later. "People left their homes, were beaten, saw no clear purpose to endure the abuse, grew bored with the protests, and returned to their homes. We had the capacity to organize people, but not to develop a strategy or political vision to lead." The ability of activists to mobilize, in the early stage of the movement, had depended on their ability to transfer the loyalty members felt toward preexisting groups to the new social movement organizations and to equate prior collective identities with high risk political activity. As time passed, however, and the regime recovered its strength and unity, activists grew weary. A 1986 survey conducted by Elizabeth Lira found 72 percent of Chileans suffering high degrees of tension; 49.9 percent wanting to leave the country for political and personal-security reasons; 66.9 percent recognizing that in the past years, they visited friends and family less; 60

percent feeling resigned and disappointed; and 44 percent feeling sad. Only 3.7 percent of Chileans expected justice in the case of the two young people burned alive (Camus and Collyer 1987, 25). As Sid Tarrow notes, at the peak of a cycle of protest, it is often more difficult to maintain enthusiasm. Movement leaders will, thus, shift to more costly, but more direct, forms of political action (Tarrow 1992b, 18).

The Chilean Communist Party's increasing emphasis on clandestine military operations, during this period, can best be understood in this light, although strategically the results were disastrous. Three days after the failed September 4, 1986 protest, the Frente Patriótico Manuel Rodríguez attempted to assassinate General Pinochet as he drove down the driveway to his house in Maipo. While the Communists celebrated the pure audacity of the attempt, the failed assassination sparked a new wave of repression against grassroots activists. Pinochet imposed a state of siege, and, within a week, four left-wing activists were pulled from their homes and assassinated (ostensibly to avenge Pinochet's four bodyguards killed by a bomb that exploded under the wrong car). The military raided the poblaciones, arresting thousands of residents, and destroying hundreds of homes. They issued orders of arrest for all shantytown leaders and routinely tortured those detained. The death toll for 1986 alone now reached two hundred.

The armed strategy cost the Party heavily, in lost alliance partners and increased repression. By the end of 1986 Chile averaged between one and two political slayings weekly, four to five frustrated homicides weekly, two torture cases daily, a thousand political arrests monthly, and ninety cases of cruel and inhuman treatment (Camus and Collyer

1987, 216). The PC's armed strategy also caused a widening gulf between the mass movement and the armed groups, and between Communist activists and shantytown residents. Political rivalries destroyed communal solidarity as party leaders tried "to prove that they had a larger base, or more force," Violeta, of Herminda, observes. By the end of the protest movement, the level of political participation had markedly declined. In Herminda even the democratic neighborhood council shattered from within. As one ex-council member explains, "We became dependent on the municipality and lost contact with the pobladores." The Communists tried to dominate the council exacerbating internal political rifts. "Finally, we had to resign. The government appointed its own neighborhood council, and all that we had done was lost."

Similarly, Chino, from Granadilla, laments:

> In the end the only thing that really mattered was whether the protests served to overthrow the dictatorship. They did not help us improve the level of organization in the población. It was like the gold rush. We had terrible illusions. The disillusion was pure torment. If you look at what we had after the protests, in comparison to what we had before the protests—community farms, soup kitchens, day care, education workshops, Minimum Employment Program workshops, everyone employed, everyone incorporated. We had over sixty people working on the farm and in the kitchen, feeding over two hundred and fifty children. We put everything at risk, because we felt that was the cost we had to pay to overthrow the dictatorship. Everything we had created, we ended up destroying. We were very heroic, of course, but what did we gain?

A lone demonstrator trying to protect the rest by kicking a tear-gas bomb away from the crowd.

CHAPTER SIX

The Transition to Democracy

The cycle of protests that began on May 11, 1983, ended abruptly in a shower of gun fire on September 7, 1986. The state of siege imposed in response to a failed assassination attempt, four revenge murders in the week that followed, thousands of arrests in the next few months, the disappearance of five young people the following year, the escalation of torture under the regime's Fiscal (public prosecutor) Torres, and the general state of fear and exhaustion in the country marked the end of the 1983–1986 protest cycle. Pinochet's lifting of the state of siege a week before the Pope's visit to Chile, in April 1987, sparked a brief revival. By May 1987, however, leaders of the moderate political parties had shifted their demand for "democracy now" to "free elections" in 1988. One noted authority on social movements observes:

> The power of protest lies neither in its numbers, nor its level of violence, but in its threat to burst through the

boundaries of the accepted limits of social behavior. . . .
The paradox is that collective actors who have only dis-
ruptive collective action as a resource, by their very actions bring it within the conventional repertoire and so
deprive themselves of its power. . . . As the repertoire of
collective action evolves in a more radical direction . . . [it]
raises the risks of collective action, divides the movements
and reduces their following, and allows elites to reestablish
order through repression and reform (Tarrow 1989b, 7–8).

In July 1987, the moderate Campaign for Free Elections became the Concertación for the No, a coalition founded to negotiate the terms of a constitutionally mandated
plebiscite on Pinochet's rule. By mid-1988, even the Communists, who had for well over a year insisted that the
plebiscite, as part of Pinochet's own constitution, was designed to demobilize the movement, not facilitate a transition to democracy, had conceded that the plebiscite was the
only remaining path for change.

The shift in strategy gave the Alianza Democrática and
political elites dominance over both the Communists and
the mobilized sectors of the popular classes. From 1983–1986,
as one social scientist observes, there had been

> two kinds of protests going on . . . [one] for the political
> elites of the Democratic alliance . . . characterized by the
> formation of a broad centrist coalition that would negoti-
> ate with the representatives of the regime . . . and [one] for
> the other [the MDP] . . . for whom street mobilization was the
> main means to end the dictatorship (Oppenheim 1993, 186).

The breach had worked in the Alianza Democrática's favor.
As General Matthei admitted, in an interview with Alfred

Stepan in January 1988, the mobilizations had led the military to fear a contested Yes vote in the plebiscite more than a defeat for the government and made them willing to negotiate the terms of transition (Stepan 1988a).

Between April and October 1988, the leaders of the Concertación and the generals negotiated the rules to govern the plebiscite campaign. By October, ten of the thirteen traditional guarantees (e.g., opposition poll watchers, voter-registration drives, media coverage) were in place. On the day of the plebiscite Santiago was tense. Residents stood in long lines at voting tables staffed with police and opposition poll watchers. At one table Javier Sáez, a leader of the Communist youth, approached a police officer. "Where are the opposition poll watchers at this table? Who is winning here?" The police officer turned with a grin, "Why the opposition is winning by 80 percent, we don't have to be enemies any more."

Throughout the day, government radio announced the government's lead. The opposition radio claimed the lead for the opposition. At 9:00 P.M. all broadcasts stopped. At the government's campaign headquarters civilian politicians engaged in fierce debate. At 12:30 A.M., Sergio Onafre Jarpa, leader of the Coalition for the Yes, suddenly appeared on television, acknowledging the government's defeat. Pinochet, still not conceding, called an emergency meeting of the generals in the Moneda. Confronted by a journalist in front of the presidential palace, Matthei confirmed the report: "The government has lost, 55 to 44 percent." The cumulative vote against Pinochet in Santiago's poorer districts was closer to 65 percent. In wealthy Las Condes, Pinochet won 75 percent of the vote. In impoverished La Pintana, he lost, 68 percent to 32 percent.

So it was, on October 7, 1988, that the mass movement, unable to defeat the regime militarily, defeated it politically. As one Chilean sociologist observed, the movement had "changed the face of [Chilean] society . . . allow[ing] people to overcome fear . . . reveal[ing] the military's failure to dissolve collective identities and inhibit collective action, and reintroduc[ing] political space for civil society" (Garretón 1986, 270). It had allowed the political parties to escape their clandestine nuclei, and citizens to openly seek the support of their political parties. It had even driven opening wedges in the military regime, convincing a sizable proportion of the officer corps that it would be unwise to try to defend the delegitimized regime against a mobilized and united populace. The 1983–1986 cycle of protests had set the stage for a negotiated transition to democracy in 1990.

The democracy Chile entered in 1990 was strikingly different from that which was overthrown in the bloody military coup of 1973. Having accepted the legitimacy of the 1980 constitution to defeat Pinochet by ballot, the Concertación was now in a bind. On the one hand, the constitution was still the Concertación's only guarantee that elections would be held in 1989. If, on the other hand, the opposition accepted the legitimacy of 1980 constitution, they would also have to limit their democratic aspirations. The 1980 constitution gave Pinochet the authority to postpone elections until December 1989, and if defeated again, to remain as acting president until March 1990. The defeated president would remain, then, as commander-and-chief of the armed forces, head of the National Security Council (made up of the Pinochet and the generals), with veto power over civilian legislation, and senator for life. The armed forces were granted broad tutelary powers to defend the nation and the institutional order and were guaranteed a budget equal to or greater than that during Pinochet's last year in office. Ten percent of all copper revenues would go directly to the armed forces, with no control levied by the civilian head of state. The constitution also prohibited Marxist parties from participating in the new democracy, designated nine, nonelected senators (one third of the new Senate) to remain in office until 1997, and forbade the incoming government to change the constitution without the approval of two-thirds of both houses of Congress and the president, in two consecutive terms.

While the Concertación challenged these undemocratic elements, they were unable to force concessions from the government. Eventually, they settled for a package of fifty-four minor constitutional reforms; only five would produce significant change.

1. The size of the Senate would be increased from twenty-six to thirty-eight members, to reduce the impact of the designated senators.

2. Article 8, prohibiting Marxist parties was to be abrogated.

3. The National Security Council would be broadened to include civilians.

4. Pinochet would remain as commander-and-chief of the armed forces, but his Senate seat would go to a retired general.

5. Most importantly, the law restricting changes in the constitution was modified to permit the president, after two-thirds approval in both houses, to amend the constitution, without resubmitting it to the next elected president and Congress.

If these modifications were approved in the July 30,

1989, plebiscite, the Concertación leaders felt confident they could make more substantial changes once they were in power. They were wrong.

Shortly after losing the plebiscite, Pinochet passed a series of binding laws (leyes amarres) designed to prevent any modification of the political or economic system. The new laws

> prevented the incoming government from replacing most of the federal bureaucracy, the heads of the Supreme Court, the Constitutional Court, and the armed forces; . . . [gave the military] powers parallel to those of the president and minister of defense; . . . privatize[d] industries; . . . and tie[d] the hands of the incoming government" (Oppenheim 1993, 209).

Most importantly, the new laws changed the rules governing elections. In contrast to the proportional representation system characteristic of pre-1973 Chile, the new electoral system mandated two-member districts, with seats split between the party or political list with the largest plurality and that with the second largest percentage of votes. Unless the largest party doubled the votes of the second largest party, the two parties would win an even number of seats. Smaller parties would receive no seats. To prevent Pinochet's candidates from winning at least half the congressional seats, then, all anti-Pinochet parties would have to run on a single list. If they failed to double the Rights's support in the congressional elections, they would not have enough seats to pass even minimal legislation.

After intense negotiation, the Concertación agreed to nominate former Senator Patricio Aylwin for president. The leaders of each political party compromised on a single slate of congressional candidates. The Christian Democrats insisted that the Communist Party be excluded from the Concertación's list, but allowed the Communists to run candidates in thirteen districts where the Socialist Party had agreed not to present candidates.

On December 14, 1989, Patricio Aylwin won the presidency with 55 percent of the vote, the same percentage the Concertación had won in the plebiscite. Hernán Büchi, Pinochet's candidate and former minister of the economy, fell far behind with 29 percent. Francisco Errazúriz, the candidate of the Centro-Centro, an independent businessman who claimed to be above politics, took home 15 percent. Because the right-wing parties also united to run on a single list, the Concertación candidates won only 72 of 120

CATHY LISA SCHNEIDER

Mothers of the disappeared marching in protest, demanding justice for their children, on the day following the election.

seats in the Chamber of Deputies and 22 of the 38 seats in the Senate. This left the Concertación one short of the required two-thirds majority in the Chamber, and, due to the designated senators, one short of a majority in the Senate. The ability of the incoming government to pass legislation would, after that, depend on the Concertación's ability to negotiate with right-wing senators and representatives.

The Communist Party did not win any congressional seats, although it won an average of 16 percent in the thirteen districts in which it had presented candidates (the same percentage it traditionally had averaged in national elections). The Party's poor showing exacerbated the divisions publicly manifested at the May 1989 Congress. The Congress, the first held in twenty years, had been the scene of bitter acrimony and recrimination. Gladys Marín had condemned the "old men" on the central committee for not supporting the *rebelión popular* more forcefully, for not sufficiently backing those risking their lives, and for abandoning the rebellion in favor of a bourgeois democratic transition. Luís Guastavino attacked Marín and her followers for left-wing adventurism, for endangering the lives of countless young activists, and for not recognizing the importance of the 1988 plebiscite in time. Internal elections failed to create peace. Marín's faction won most central committee seats. Volodia Teitelboim, a former parliamentarian noted for his ability to negotiate, became the new general secretary. Even Teitelboim, however, was unable to prevent the rapid unraveling of the Chilean Communist Party, as it witnessed the collapse of seven Eastern European regimes by November of 1989.

In the months that followed, Chilean communists fought over interpretations of the collapse of Socialist Europe; the meaning of democracy; the failure of the peaceful road to socialism; the failure of the rebelión popular; the new democratic government; and the future of the Frente, the militias, and armed struggle. The party's poor electoral showing in December of 1989 was the final blow. Within a few months, Guastavino's faction had deserted the Party, forming the Asamblea de Renovación Comunista (ARCO, Assembly of Communist Renovation). By December of 1990 the Communist Party had virtually disappeared. Two of its factions joined separate factions of the Socialist Party, ARCO became the Party of the Independent Left (modeled along the lines of the Italian ex-communists), and a more extreme faction joined the Frente Autónomo (formed by members of the Frente Patriótico Manuel Rodríguez who had broken with the Party in 1988). Only one faction remained as the Communist Party of Chile. By 1994, that faction was headed by Marín.

While the debates had ripped the Communist Party into five distinct factions, the eight factions of the Socialist Party converged, encouraged by their need to compete with the Christian Democrats for authority within the Concertación. Having reached the conclusion that the stability of Chilean democracy depended on the endurance of a center-left coalition, as represented by the Concertación, and having accepted the free market, limited democracy, and export-led growth, the Socialists found it difficult to distinguish themselves from the Christian Democrats. Unwilling to challenge the Christian Democrats by rallying the Left or mobilizing the poor, several Socialist leaders tried to convey an image of modernity and technical expertise.

By the time the democratic government took office, the tone of political debate had been altered radically. As Julia Paley cogently observes:

changes in the legitimation of knowledge were so powerful that they structured not only the work of free marketeers
but the work of those who opposed neoliberal economic
and military rule as well . . . alter[ing] relations of power
by delegitimizing the voices and knowledge of Chileans
without doctoral degrees . . . and remov[ing] economic
policy from political debate (Paley 1994, 145–147).

While political structure and popular culture had been
mutually reinforcing before 1973, the structure of incentives in the new democracy undermined traditional collective identities and dispositions. Before 1973, for instance,
proportional representation encouraged political parties to
compete for support of the urban poor and, in so doing,
stimulated the growth of highly politicized grassroots organizations. Political competition among elites, thus, made it
possible for shantytown residents to mobilize successfully
to obtain housing and services.

Although the 1973 coup destroyed the left-wing political parties, the structure of power in the new dictatorship
preserved the popular culture of the Chilean Left. As Paley
observes:

In his attempt to eliminate organizing among the urban
poor, Pinochet actually created space for mass organizing
in the poblaciones because he made conflict a phenomenon of daily life. By constituting poor people as
subversives, by defining social relations as a war, and by
establishing an atmosphere of patriots vs. enemies, the
dictator created an antagonistic environment conducive
to rebellion. . . . The construction of Pinochet as the
symbolic cause of misery facilitated vast mobilizations in
the shantytowns" (Paley 1994, 169–170).

The lack of legal channels favored clandestine party activity and strong grassroots networks, while high unemployment rates guaranteed clandestine parties a steady stream of dedicated cadres, with the time to devote to full-time party work.

The activist popular culture of the shantytowns, in turn, saved the left-wing political parties from extinction. The explosion of protests set loose by the 1983 economic crisis catapulted the political parties back into the public arena and channeled a new stream of resources to the urban poor. Finally, the protests paved the way for a transition to democratic rule. The structure of the new democracy, ironically, stripped the poor of political resources, removing "the leadership base for future movement activists" (Tarrow 1992b, 25). Forced to compete for the support of the Right; fearful of the mobilization of the Left; and dependent on the cooperation of businessman, Right-wing senators, and the military, the governing parties no longer needed grassroots activists. As one political scientist notes:

> Because Aylwin and his advisers wanted to avoid engaging in confrontational politics, they were leery about using popular mobilization as a way to pressure the Right. This left unresolved the issue of how to ensure popular participation in fundamental political decisions. . . . [This] resulted in a lack of connection between the grassroots, on the one hand, and party and government elites on the other (Oppenheim 1993, 214, 227).

Many ardent grassroots activists felt abandoned and betrayed by the new democracy. As one Socialist shantytown organizer bitterly remarked:

> While we were struggling, party leaders were living

abroad. It was we who went to jail, were tortured by the CNI, lost our jobs and our loved ones. Now they are back in control, but they won't lower themselves to ask about our concerns. No, they've returned to politics as usual. All of the party leaders are the same, they do what they want, they don't concern themselves with our needs.

In the end, seventeen years of resistance work had cost the grassroots activists heavily. Of those who escaped death, few had escaped torture. Throughout the dictatorship their only goal had been political change. They had neglected their educations, their families, their careers. Now, with a seventeen year gap in their resumes and families to support, they had lost their only livelihood. Many succumbed to what Chilean psychologists have labeled "a state of numbness," a consequence of living most of their lives under constant threat of death.

For the grassroots activists, seventeen years of persecution, torture, and fear had proven the danger of pursuing, with too much ardor, a political position that could be defeated, or proven wrong. As one former Communist lamented:

I dedicated my life to politics, I sacrificed everything for what I believed. I was tortured, my friends were killed, and my family spent almost twenty years in poverty. In the end everything I believed in was false. I don't want to pay such a price to be wrong again.

Even the least active shantytown dwellers were affected by this culture of fear. As an old woman in Sara Gajardo explained:

You don't know what we suffered. There were bodies everywhere, the Mapocho river was full of bodies. You

CATHY LISA SCHNEIDER

A confrontation with police near the city jail.

think the big monopolies are just going to stand by and let the government take them over. That's why I say there's going to be another coup. That's why I hate the Communists. That's why I won't let my son get involved in politics. That's why I'm terrified every time my sons are in the streets.

Seventeen years of economic crisis, high unemployment rates, and spates of bankruptcies had also convinced labor organizers and the rank-and-file that if they pushed too hard they risked everything. They had watched their friends and comrades die in the coup of 1973. They had watched companies go bankrupt and workers lose their jobs between 1973 and 1982. For those who lived long enough to witness the 1983–1992 economic recovery a profound re-evaluation had occurred. As a worker in a fishmeal factory told Duncan Green: "I feel real anxiety about the future.

They can chuck you out at any time; you can't think five years ahead. If you've got money, you can get an education and health care. Money is everything here now" (Green 1994, 140).

The changes in the structure of the economy complemented the transformation of the political system, atomizing and depoliticizing popular identities and culture. After 1983, under Pinochet's new economic minister Hernán Büchi, Chile pursued an aggressive economic policy, "centered around export-led growth and based on low wages, a high level of internal oligopoly, and a flexible labor market with severe restrictions on unions" (Díaz 1993, 22). The economic recovery was accompanied by a notable increase in social inequalities. The richest decile, which in 1978 controlled 37 percent of national income, in 1988, controlled 47 per cent. The income of the poorest decile, during the same period, dropped from 20 to 17 percent, leaving 5.2 million Chileans, 40.1 percent of the population, in poverty. Three years later, in spite of the transition to democracy with all the freedoms of association that that implied, and despite "the increase in the real incomes of workers and of the poorest 40 per cent of the population, there was no significant change in the distribution of national and personal income" (Díaz 1993, 23–24).

By 1992, Chile had the third fastest growing economy in the world. "Per capita GDP grew by almost a fifth, exports by 14 percent, and investment rose from under 19 percent of GDP to an impressive 27 percent, unmatched anywhere except by the Asian tigers" (Green 1994, 13). Inflation dropped below 20 percent and unemployment fell below 5 percent. Underemployment and casual employment, however, continued to swell, and wages lagged below their 1970 level.

Export-led growth depended on this low-wage labor. Even in 1993, only 20 percent of Chile's exports were in manufactured goods. Jobs in seasonal agriculture were largely held by women who worked for minimal wages, had no organizational representation, and no history or familiarity with labor organizing.

The shift from an economy based on large industrial firms to one of large conglomerate chains called AFP's (mutual funds), which currently manage one third of Chile's GNP and subcontract out to medium-sized, small, and *microempresas* (firms with less than four employees that, by 1990, accounted for over 45 percent of the work force), has reduced the 1990 ratio of workers to employers to half that of 1960 (Van Hemelryck 1992, 154) and severely weakened labor's clout. The owners of such small enterprises often live on the verge of poverty, dependent on temporary contracts. While the ten richest families control the AFP's, workers in microempresas are paid salaries barely above subsistence, without fringe benefits or job security. Chile's new labor regulations encourage this "flexibility," which government leaders believe is responsible for Chile's spectacular growth rates. As one well-respected economist notes:

> Precarious waged employment constitutes the single most important element of poverty in present-day Chile. . . . This precariousness is manifested in low levels of job stability, dependence upon income from piecework, poor working conditions, rigid specialization at work, little access to training, few possibilities for internal mobility in the company, impediments to collective negotiation, low levels of participation and, sometimes, subjection to authoritarian relations in the workplace (Díaz 1993, 23–24).

The precarious and temporary nature of employment in Chile's new democracy has abated the promise of collective action. "A labor force once accustomed to secure unionized jobs," notes Duncan Green, "has been turned into a collection of anxious individualists" (Green 1994, 140). Whether they own a small, precarious business, or subcontract their labor on a temporary basis, Chileans now work alone. They have little contact with other workers, or neighbors, and only limited time with their families. Their exposure to political or labor organizers is minimal and except for some important public-service sectors, such as health care, they lack the resources or the disposition to challenge the state. Irregular hours, unstable employment, and low caloric intake have increased levels of physical and mental exhaustion. The number of serious injuries in the workplace tripled between 1980 and 1990 (Díaz 1992, 117).

This fragmentation of public and private social relations also has obscured the sense of collective fate and identity among Chile's working class (Díaz 1992, 117). Díaz notes:

> There has been a displacement from the neighborhood and the street to the workplace; from relationships with neighbors to relationships with clients; from a relationship with the administrator of the emergency employment program to one with a private entrepreneur. Work hours have changed, family relations have been modified, and the quantity of social interactions have multiplied (Díaz 1992, 117).

By 1990, surveys of Chilean citizens revealed a sharp drop in the number of ideologically predisposed individuals (Waugh 1990, 20-30). In comparison to 1972, when

only 10.7 percent of the respondents did not place themselves on the ideological scale and only 19.7 percent did
not identify with a political party, . . . in the three recent
surveys [since 1989] the mean of those who did not identify with a particular ideological orientation jumped to 31.4
percent, while the mean for those who did not identify
with a political party jumped to a whopping 65.8 percent.
. . . This suggests that the massification of the center does
not so much indicate ideological moderation (i.e., a conscious change in belief systems and values of many to
favor a more centrist or specifically Christian Democratic
philosophy), . . . [as it suggests that] a substantial percentage of the population is not much interested in politics,
nor is ideology a useful cognitive tool for them in organizing and understanding political information...the authoritarian experience has induced a degree of political
formlessness in Chilean society (Waugh 1990, 20–30).

In the 1992 municipal elections, for example, the strongest determinant was incumbency. Fifty-one percent of the
pobladores said they had little interest, and 27 percent no
interest, in the municipal election campaign (Hagopian 1994,
8; Centro de Estudios de la Realidad Contemporánea 1992,
5). There was also a dramatic decline in party membership.
Arriagada, for instance, noted that the DC, which had ten
electors for every militant in 1969, had fifty-five by 1992
(cited by Hagopian 1994, 8; see also Arriagada n.d.).

Several things about the Chilean experience are perti-
nent for students of social movements. Most importantly,
the Chilean case demonstrates the integral and reinforcing
quality of the relationship between politics and urban social
movements. As Castells observes, "the level and meaning

of community organizations are essentially determined by the political system and by the characteristics of the political agent to which squatters relate" (Castells 1983, 210). In Chile, the shantytown resistance movement was shaped by the historical link between particular urban neighborhoods and the Communist party. In neighborhoods without this long left-wing tradition, community organizations, like those in Lo Hermida, did little more than help residents survive from one crisis to another. These neighborhoods were extremely vulnerable to military repression. In Sara Gajardo, for instance, residents observed that military shelling focused against Herminda de la Victoria resulted in more fatalities in their own población. In Villa O'Higgens even the local parish provided no direction, because it received none from members of the community.

In all highly mobilized poblaciones—Pablo Neruda, Yungay, Herminda de la Victoria, La Victoria, Granadilla—the Chilean Communist Party was deeply integrated in the población, and party activists were an important part of the neighborhood's social fabric. In Pablo Neruda, young people led the resistance struggles. Yet, they understood their activity as the continuation of the struggles that had characterized their community since its inception. In La Victoria, older grassroots militants were still an important part of the struggle. Although too old to engage in protest, older militants served as role models and guides to younger activists. In Yungay, communal solidarity, radical militancy, and common ideology boosted the población to reclaim democratic spaces and effectively assert community control.

Individual activists did not determine the extent or success of protest action. Activists were often killed or arrested and were replaced by youths who found themselves heirs to the same tradition. What was important was the extent to which community solidarity and a widely shared political vision had made its members potential activists. Tarrow cogently observes:

> Organizations develop only to the extent that a mobilization potential in the society gives them a popular foundation. Their survival depends upon their success in creating a resonance between the culture of their mass base and their own ideologies and strategies (Tarrow 1989b, 15).

Protests, therefore, clustered in Communist neighborhoods, where decades of local organizing efforts had left a strong solidary network of experienced grassroots activists and a culture of collective opposition.

At its best, then, the Communist Party functioned as a source of political culture and direction, distilling the essence of each neighborhood's experience and creativity. At its worst, the Party attempted to exert hegemony over the movement, losing contact with its base in the process.

We see this tension very clearly in the fate of the neighborhood council in Herminda de la Victoria, its failure, a direct consequence of the Communist Party's attempt to exert hegemonic control. As a member of the neighborhood council commented: "We lost contact with the pobladores. . . . We began to divide among ourselves. . . . The PC simply wanted to dominate the council."

Only where activists addressed the needs and concerns of local residents were they able to maintain a constant level of resistance.

We see a similar phenomenon in the university-student movement. In the first phase of student unrest (1978–1981), the Communist Party maintained an open, democratic relationship with the student body, including students from the movement in the decision-making process and turning the entire campus into an open assembly. In the second phase (after 1983), however, the political parties began to compete for hegemony, using the students as pawns in their national strategy. As a result, the second phase of the student movement was much weaker and more fragmented than the first.

There is, also, ample evidence to support the political process model. Protests began in solidary grassroots communities where a history of successful political organizing had forged strong activist networks and a culture of collective opposition. A shift in the political opportunity structure brought on by the 1982 economic crisis allowed clandestine political activists to reach beyond these communities and recruit a broader array of citizens. As the movement reached a peak, its leaders employed a more inclusive and less partisan discourse. Protests became widespread, diluting the intensity of the bond between the original movement activists. "The more inclusive the collective identity," contends McAdam, "the harder it is to control, and thus the less powerful it is as a collective incentive" (McAdam 1992, 163).

Finally, competition between social actors encouraged more extreme and violent protest actions. The more moderate movement leaders used the threat of extremism to convince the state to hold a plebiscite in 1988. Pinochet's defeat marked the end of the protest movement. Tarrow notes:

> As tactical innovation leads to violent clashes and repression, the enthusiasm and energy of the earlier period give way to bitterness and exhaustion. Some participants de-

fect; others organize to commit violent acts; and divisions arise between the more and less militant groups—divisions which demoralize participants, allow authorities an entering wedge, and hasten the end of mobilization (Tarrow 1989b, 7–8).

What, then, is likely to be the future of Chile? The dramatic structural changes that have occurred over the past two decades make it difficult to imagine a political actor capable of mobilizing widespread support. Yet, all movements experience a demobilization and a decline. "What we remember most," writes Aristide Zolberg, "is that moments of political enthusiasm are followed by bourgeois repression or by charismatic authoritarianism, sometimes by horror, but always by the restoration of boredom" (Zolberg 1972, 205 cited by Tarrow 1994, 172). Similarly, economist Albert Hirschman cites a "rebound effect" where those individuals most fiercely committed to the struggle "return to private life with a degree of disgust proportional to the effort they have extended" (Tarrow 1994, 172; see also Hirschman 1982, 80). If we ignore these common cyclical aspects of social movements, Alessandro Pizzorno warns, "at every upstart of a wave we shall be induced to think that we are at the verge of a revolution: and when the downswing appears we shall predict the end of class conflict" (1978, 291). Perhaps, then, Chile is simply in a period of transition and reflux. The deep rooted opposition political culture and the networks of resistance that allowed Chileans to mobilize against authoritarian rule may only be in hiatus.

In August 1994, President Frei submitted five constitutional amendments to the Senate that would have:

1. eliminated the appointment of senators;

CATHY LISA SCHNEIDER

Young people celebrating the defeat of Pinochet's candidate and the victory of the democratic forces.

2. changed the binominal electoral system to a corrected proportional system;

3. expanded the Chamber of Deputies' powers;

4. expanded the Constitutional Court; and

5. expanded presidential powers to include the right to call a plebiscite.

These measures would have substantially restructured political opportunities in Chile. Although they were defeated, the current structure of the Chilean government will automatically be challenged in 1997, when the nine designated senators' terms expire and the president of the republic's power to name the new heads of the armed forces will be returned. These measures will strengthen the government's ability to enact further reforms, eventually, perhaps, making it expedient for political parties to mobilize the poor. Under these conditions, long dormant sentiments and identities may suddenly reawaken, and Chile will again be shaken by an apocalypse of popular rebellion.

BIBLIOGRAPHY

Ad Hoc Working Group of the United Nations. 1975. *Report of the Economic and Social Council* A–1028.

Agurto, Irene; Manuel Canales; Gonzalo de la Masa. 1985. *La juventud Chilena: Razones y subversiones.* Santiago: Eco/Folico/Sepade.

Allende, Isabel. 1986. *House of the Spirits.* New York: Bantam Books.

Alvarado, Luis; Rosemond Cheetham; and Jaime Rojas. 1973. "Movilización social en torno al problema de vivienda." *Revista Latinoamericana de estudios urbanos regionales* 7.

Alvarez, Pedro Guzman. 1982. Letter written while *alcalde* (mayor) of La Granja to the director of the Servicio de la Vivienda y Urbanismo (Housing and Urban Development), ord. no. 788 (June 25).

Alvarez, Sonia E. 1990. *Engendering Democracy in Brazil: Women's Movements in Transition Politics.* Princeton: Princeton University Press.

Americas' Watch. 1983. "Chile since the Coup: Ten Years of Repression." New York (April 25).

————. 1988 *Chile: Human Rights and the Plebiscite*. New York (July).

Anderson, Benedict. 1983. *Imagined Communities: Reflections on the Origin and Spread of Nationalism*. London: Verso.

Angell, Alan. 1972. *Politics and the Labour Movement in Chile*. New York: Oxford University Press.

————. 1991. "Unions and Workers in Chile during the 1980s." Pp. 188–211, in *The Struggle for Democracy in Chile, 1982–1990*, ed. Paul W. Drake and Ivan Jaksic. Lincoln: University of Nebraska Press.

Angell, Alan and Benny Pollack. 1990. "The Chilean Elections of 1989 and the Politics of the Transition to Democracy." *Bulletin of Latin American Research* 9, no. 1: 1–23.

Arellano, José Pablo. 1987. "La situación social in Chile." Corporación de Investigaciones Económicas para América Latina, Notas técnica 94. Santiago: Corporación de Investigaciones Económicas para América Latina (CIEPLAN).

Arrate, Jorge. 1986. *La fuerza democrática de la idea socialista*. Santiago: Las Ediciones del Ornitorrinco.

Arriagada, Genaro. 1985. *La política militar de Pinochet*. Santiago: Salesianos.

————. 1988. *Pinochet: The Politics of Power*, trans. Nancy Morris, Vincent Ercolano, and Kristen A. Whitney. Boston: Allen and Unwin.

————. (n.d.) "Carta a los militantes: La reforma del Estado del Partido." Internal memo.

Avello, David Jesús et al., eds. 1989. *Constructores de ciudad: Nueve historias del primer concurso historias de las poblaciones*. Santiago: Ediciones Sur.

Baloyra, Enrique A., ed. 1987. *Comparing Democracies: Transition and Consolidation in Mediterranean Europe and the Southern Cone*. Boulder, Colo.: Westview Press.

Baño, Rodrigo. 1985. *Lo social y lo político*. Santiago: Facultad Latinoamericana de Ciencias Sociales (hereafter referred to as FLACSO).

Barnard, Andrew. 1970. "Chilean Communists, Radical Presidents, and Chilean Relations with the United States: 1940–1947." *Journal of Latin American Studies* 13, no. 2.

———. 1978. *The Chilean Communist Party, 1922–1947*. Ph.D. diss., University College, London.

Barrera, Manuel and Gonzalo Falabella. 1989. *Sindicatos bajo regímenes militares: Argentina, Brasil, Chile*. Santiago: Centro de Estudios Sociales (hereafter referred to as CES).

Barría, Jorge S. 1971. "Perspectiva histórica de la huelga obrera in Chile." *Cuadernos de la realidad nacional* 9 (September): 119–155.

Barros Gatica, Jaime. 1989. *Deindustrialization in Chile*. Boulder, Colo.: Westview Press.

Benavides, Leopoldo; Eduardo Morales; and Sergio Rojas. 1983. "Campamentos y poblaciones en las comunas de gran Santiago. Un síntesis informativa." Documento de trabajo. No. 192. Santiago: FLACSO.

Bengoa, José; Javier Martínez; and Eugenio Tironi, eds. 1987. *Marginalidad, movimientos sociales, y democracia, Proposiciones* 14. Santiago: Ediciones Sur.

Bergquist. Charles W. 1986. *Labor in Latin America: Comparative Essays on Chile, Argentina, Venezuela, and Colombia.* Stanford: Stanford University Press.

Bermeo, Nancy. 1990. "Rethinking Regime Change." *Comparative Politics* 22, no. 3 (April): 359–374.

Bitar, Sergio. 1987. Interviewed in *Análisis* (May 9–15).

Borzutzky, Silvia T. 1987. "The Pinochet Regime: Crisis and Consolidation." In *Authoritarians and Democrats: Regime Transition in Latin America,* ed. James M. Malloy and Mitchell A. Seligson. Pittsburgh: University of Pittsburgh Press.

Brodsky, Ricardo and Ramiro Pizarro. 1985. "La constitución del movimiento estudiantil como proceso de aprendizaje político." In *La juventud Chilena: Razones y subversiones,* ed. Irene Agurto, Manuel Canales, and Gonzalo de la Maza. Santiago: Eco/Folico/Sepade.

Brown, Cynthia. 1980. "The High Cost of Monetarism in Chile." *The Nation* (September 27).

Buchanan, Albert. 1980. "Revolutionary Motivation and Rationality." In *Marx, Justice, and History,* ed. Marshall Cohen, Thomas Nagel, and Thomas Scanlon. Princeton: Princeton University Press.

Budnik, Miguel. 1986. *Los marginados.* Santiago. Empresa Editora Araucaria.

Burbach, Roger. 1989. "Chile: A Requiem for the Left?" Unpublished paper.

Calderon, Fernando, ed. 1986. *Los movimientos sociales ante la crisis*. Buenos Aires: Centro Latinoamericano de Ciencias Sociales.

Campero, Guillermo. 1987. *Entre la sobrevivencia y la acción política: La organizaciones de pobladores en Santiago*. Santiago: Ediciones Instituto Latinoamericano de Estudios Transnacionales.

―――. 1989. "El movimiento sindical en el capitalismo autoritario: Un intento de reflexión y perspectiva." Pp. 175–219 in *Sindicatos bajo regímenes militares: Argentina, Brasil, Chile*. ed. Manuel Barrera and Gonzalo Falabella. Santiago: CES.

Camus, María Eugenia and Patricia Collyer. 1987. "¿Estamos locos los Chilenos?" *Análisis* (February 3–7): 25–29.

Carnoy, Martin. 1984. *The State and Political Theory*. Princeton: Princeton University Press.

Carr, Barry and Steve Ellner, eds. 1993. *The Latin American Left: From the Fall of Allende to Perestroika*. Boulder, Colo.: Westview Press and London: Latin American Bureau.

Castells, Manuel. 1973. "Movimiento de pobladores y lucha de clases." Cuadro No 2. *Revista Latinoamericana de estudios urbanos regionales* (April): 9–35.

―――. 1983. *The City and the Grassroots: A Cross-Cultural Theory of Urban Social Movements*. Berkeley and Los Angeles: University of California Press.

Cavarozzi, Marcelo. 1992. "Pattern of Elite Negotiation and Confrontation in Argentina and Chile." In *Elites and Democratic Consolidation in Latin America and Southern Europe*, ed. Richard Gunther and John Higley. Cambridge: Cambridge University Press.

Centro de Estudios del Desarrollo. 1990. *Dos ciudades: Análisis de la estructura socio-económica-espacial del gran-Santiago*. Santiago: Centro de Estudios del Desarrollo (hereafter referred to as CED).

Centro de Estudios de la Realidad Contemporánea. 1989. "Informe encuesta nacional." Santiago: Universidad Academia de Humanismo Cristiano.

—————. 1992. "Informe de prensa: Encuesta gran Santiago" (June).

Centro de Estudios de Trabajo. 1983. *Páginas sindicales: Tercera y cuarta protestas*. Ano 6, numero 57, Documentación de trabajo de circulación interna, privada. Santiago: Centro de Estudios de Trabajo (Cetra/Ceal).

Chateau, Jorge et al. 1987. *Espacio y poder, los pobladores*. Santiago: FLACSO.

Chossudovsky, Michael. 1979. "Human Rights, Health, and Capital Accumulation in the Third World." *International Journal of Health Services* 9, no. 1.

Chuchryk, Patricia M. 1991. "Feminist Anti-Authoritarian Politics: The Role of Women's Organizations in the Chilean Transition to Democracy." In *The Women's Movement in Latin America: Feminism and the Transition to Democracy*, ed. Jane S. Jaquette. Boulder, Colo.: Westview Press.

Collier, David. ed. 1979. *The New Authoritarianism in Latin America*. Princeton: Princeton University Press.

Collier, Ruth Berins and David Collier. 1991. *Shaping the Political Arena*. Princeton: Princeton University Press.

Commission on Truth and Reconciliation. 1991. *La nación* (March).

Constable, Pam and Arturo Valenzuela. 1986. "Is Chile Next?" *Foreign Policy* 63.

————. 1991. *Chile under Pinochet: A Nation of Enemies*. New York: W.W. Norton.

Corradi, Juan E.; Patricia Weiss Fagen; and Manuel Antonio Garretón. 1992. *Fear at the Edge: State Terror and Resistance in Latin America*. Berkeley and Los Angeles: University of California Press.

Corvalan, Luis. 1977. "La Iglesia vista por Corvalan." Interviewed in *Excelsior*, 7 (Mexico City).

Cuadernos de economía. 1982. "Inflación persistente, inflación reprimida, y hiperinflación." *Cuadernos de economía* 43, Santiago.

Dahse, Fernando. 1979. *El mapa de la extrema riqueza*. Santiago: Editorial Acongua.

Davies, James C. 1969. "The J-curve of Rising and Declining Satisfactions as a Cause of Some Great Revolutions and a Contained Rebellion." In *Violence in America: Historical and Comparative Perspectives*, ed. Hugh Davis Graham and Ted Robert Gurr. Washington: U.S. Government Printing Office.

De la Maza, G. and Mario Garcés. 1985. *La explosión de la mayorías: Protesta nacional, 1983–1984.* Santiago: Educación y Comunicaciones.

Debray, Regis. 1967. *Revolution in the Revolution? Armed Struggle and Political Struggle in Latin America,* trans. Bobby Ortiz. New York: Monthly Review Press.

Departamento de Agricultura de Chile. 1982. *The Modernization of National Agricultural Activities: The First Stage, The Agriculture of the Chilean Government 1973–1980.* 37.

DeShazo, Peter. 1983. *Urban Workers and Labor Unions in Chile: 1902–1927.* Madison: University of Wisconsin Press.

Diamond, Larry; Juan J. Linz; and Seymour Martin Lipset. 1989. *Democracy in Developing Countries: Latin America.* Boulder, Colo.: Lynne Rienner.

Díaz, Alvaro. 1991. "Nuevas tendencias en la estructura social Chilena. Asalariación informal y pobreza en los ochenta." Pp. 88–119 in *Nacional Populismo, Voto Cambiante, Centro Político, Empleo Precario, Pequeño Empresariado, Identidad Cultural, Biotecnología,* ed. Eduardo Valenzuela, *Proposiciones* 20. Santiago: Ediciones Sur.

————. 1993. "Restructuring and the New Working Classes in Chile: Trends in Waged Employment, Informality, and Poverty, 1973–1990." United Nations Research Instituted for Social Development.

Dinges, John and Saul Landau. 1980. *Assassination on Embassy Row.* New York: Pantheon.

Dornbusch, Rudiger and Sebastian Edwards. 1991. *The Macroeconomics of Populism in Latin America*. Chicago: University of Chicago Press.

Drake, Paul W. 1978. *Socialism and Populism in Chile, 1932–1952*. Urbana: University of Illinois Press.

Drake, Paul W. and Ivan Jaksic. eds. 1991. *The Struggle for Democracy in Chile 1982–1990*. Lincoln: University of Nebraska Press.

Duarte, Gonzalo. 1986. Interview by author. Santiago, December.

Eckstein, Susan, ed. 1989. *Power and Popular Protest: Latin American Social Movements*. Berkeley and Los Angeles: University of California Press.

Eisenger, Peter K. 1973. "The Conditions of Protest Behavior in American Cities." *American Political Science Review* 67, no. 1 (March): 11–28.

Eisenstadt, S. N. 1992. "The Breakdown of Communist Regimes." *Daedalus* 121, no. 2 (Spring): 21–43.

Ellner, Steve. 1989. "The Latin American Left since Allende: Perspectives and New Directions." *Latin American Research Review* 24, no 2.

Emirbayer, Mustafa and Jeff Goodwin. 1993. "Network Analysis and Historical Sociology: The Problem of Agency." Working paper. New York: Center for the Study of Social Change, New School for Social Research.

Escobar, Arturo and Sonia Alvarez. eds. 1992. *The Making of Social Movements in Latin America: Identity, Strategy, and Democracy*, Boulder, Colo.: Westview Press.

Espinosa, Juan Guillermo. 1981. *Economic Democracy: Workers Participation in Chilean Industry 1970–1973*. New York: Academic Press.

Espinosa, Vicente. 1988. *Para una historia de los pobres de la ciudad*. Santiago: Ediciones Sur.

————. (n.d.). Interpretación de la historia reciente de los pobladores." Unpublished paper.

Evans, Peter; Dietrich Rueschemeyer; and Theda Skocpol, eds. 1985. *Bringing the State Back In*. New York: Cambridge University Press.

Evers, Tilman. 1985. "Identity: The Hidden Side of New Social Movements in Latin America." In *New Social Movements and the State in Latin America*, ed. David Slater. Dordrecht, The Netherlands: Foris Publications.

Falabella, Gonzalo. 1989. "La diversidad en el movimiento sindical Chileno bajo el régimen militar." Pp. 219–282 in *Sindicatos bajo regímenes militares: Argentina, Brasil, Chile*, ed. Manuel Barrera and Gonzalo Falabella. Santiago: CES.

Fantasia, Rick. 1988. *Cultures of Solidarity: Consciousness, Action, and Contemporary American Workers*. Berkeley and Los Angeles: University of California Press.

Faundez, Julio. 1988. *Marxism and Democracy in Chile*. New Haven: Yale University Press.

Ferree, Myra Marx. 1992. "The Political Context of Rationality: Rational Choice Theory and Resource Mobilization." In *Frontiers in Social Movement Theory*, ed.

Aldon D. Morris and Carol McClurg Mueller. New Haven: Yale University Press.

Feuer, Lewis S. ed. 1959. *Marx and Engels: Basic Writings on Politics and Philosophy*. New York: Doubleday.

Ffrench Davis, Ricardo. 1983. "The Monetarist Experiment in Chile: A Critical Survey." *World Development* 11.

Ffrench Davis, Ricardo and Dagmar Raczynski. 1990. "The Impact of Global Recession and National Policies on Living Standards: Chile, 1973–1989." Santiago: Corporación de Investigaciones Económicas para América Latina, 37.

Fleet, Michael. 1985. *The Rise and Fall of Christian Democracy*. Princeton: Princeton University Press.

Flisfisch, Angel. 1989. *La política como compromiso democrático*. Santiago: FLACSO.

Foweraker, Joe. 1989. *Making Democracy in Spain: Grass-Roots Struggle in the South 1955–1975*. Cambridge: Cambridge University Press.

Foxley, Alejandro. 1983. *Latin American Experiments in Neo-Conservative Economics*. Berkeley and Los Angeles: University of California Press.

Frias, Patricio. 1989. *El movimiento sindical Chileno en la lucha por la democracia*. Santiago: Programa de Economía del Trabajo (hereafter referred to as PET).

Friedman, Debra and Doug McAdam. 1992. "Collective Identity and Activism: Networks, Choices, and the Life of a Social Movement." In *Frontiers in Social*

Movement Theory, ed. Aldon D. Morris and Carol McClurg Mueller. New Haven: Yale University Press.

Friedman, John. 1989. "The Latin American Barrio Movement as a Social Movement: Contribution to a Debate." International Journal of Urban and Regional Research 13, no. 3: 501–510.

Friedman, John and Mauricio Salguero. 1988. "The Barrio Economy and Collective Self-Empowerment in Latin America: A Framework and Agenda for Research." In Power, Community and the City, ed. Michael Peter Smith. Comparative Urban and Community Research, vol. 1. New Brunswick, N.J.: Transaction Books.

Frühling, Hugo. 1984. "Repressive Policies and Legal Dissent in Authoritarian Regimes: Chile 1973–1981." International Journal of Law and Sociology 12, no. 4: 351–374.

Furci, Carmelo. 1984. The Chilean Communist Party and the Road to Socialism. London: Zed Books.

Gamson, William A. 1975. The Strategy of Social Protest. Homewood, Ill.: Dorsey Press.

———. 1992. Talking Politics. Cambridge: Cambridge University Press.

Garretón, Manuel Antonio. 1983. El proceso político Chileno. Santiago: FLACSO.

———. 1984. Dictaduras y democratización. Santiago: Ediciones Minga.

———. 1986. "The Political Evolution of the Chilean

Military Regime." in *Latin America*, vol.2 of *Transitions from Authoritarian Rule*, ed. Guillermo O'Donnell, Philippe C. Schmitter, and Laurence Whitehead. Baltimore: John Hopkins University Press.

————. 1989. "Popular Mobilization and the Military Regime in Chile: The Complexities of the Invisible Transition." In *Power and Popular Protest: Latin American Social Movements*, ed. Susan Eckstein. Berkeley and Los Angeles: University of California Press.

Gitlin, Todd. 1987. *The Sixties: Years of Hope, Days of Rage*. New York: Bantam Books.

Giusti, J. 1971. "La formación de las poblaciones en Santiago: Aproximación al problema de la organización de los pobladores." *Revista Latinoamericana de ciencia política*.

Goldfrank, Benjamin. 1993. *Ownership of Partnership: The Chilean Communist Party in Shantytowns of Santiago*. Honors thesis, Department of Social Studies, Harvard University.

Goldrich, Daniel. 1970. "Political Organization and the Politicization of the Poblador." *Comparative Political Studies* 3, no. 2 (July): 176–202.

Goldrich, Daniel; Raymond Pratt; and C.R. Schuller. 1967–1968. "The Political Integration of Lower Class Settlements in Chile and Peru." *Studies in Comparative and International Development* 3, no. 1: 3–22.

Goldstone, Jack. 1993. "Is Revolution Individually Rational? Groups and Individuals in Revolutionary Collective Action." Unpublished paper.

———. 1994. "Revolutions in Modern Dictatorships." In *Revolutions: Theoretical, Comparative, and Historical Studies*, ed. Jack Goldstone. Fort Worth, Texas: Harcourt Brace Jovanovich.

Gómez, María Soledad. 1988. "Factores nacionales e internacionales de la política interna del Partido Comunista de Chile (1922–1982)." in *El Partido Comunista en Chile*, ed. Augusto Varas. Santiago: FLACSO.

González, Luis E. 1985. "Transición y partidos en Chile y Uruguay." Centro de Investigaciones Sociológicas del Uruguay (Montevideo).

Graham, Hugh Davis and Ted Robert Gurr. eds. 1969. *Violence in America: Historical and Comparative Perspectives*, Washington: U.S. Government Printing Office.

Gramsci, Antonio. 1957. *The Modern Prince*. New York: International Publishers.

———. 1971. *Selections from the Prison Notebooks*. New York: International Publishers.

Granovetter, Mark S. 1973. "The Strength of Weak Ties." *American Journal of Sociology* 78, no. 6.

Green, Duncan. 1994. "Chile: The First Latin American Tiger?" *North American Congress on Latin America Report on the Americas: Mexico out of Balance* 29, no. 1 (July/August).

Grossi, Juan Rodríguez. 1985. *La distribución del ingreso y el gasto social en Chile—1983*. Santiago: Instituto

Latinoamericano de Doctrina y Estudios Sociales, Editorial Salesiana.

Gunther, Richard and John Higley. 1992. *Elites and Democratic Consolidation in Latin America and Southern Europe*. Cambridge: Cambridge University Press.

Hagopian, Frances. 1994. "State Retreat and the Reformulation of Political Representation in Latin America." Prepared for delivery at the 1994 annual meeting of the American Political Science Association, New York (September 1–4).

Hardy, Clarissa. 1984. *Los talleres artesanales de Conchalí: La organización, su recorrido y sus protagonistas*. Santiago, PET.

———. 1986. *Hambre y dignidad: Ollas comunes*. Santiago: PET.

———. 1987. *Organizarse para vivir: Pobreza urbana y organización popular*. Santiago: PET.

Hechos urbanos: Boletín de información y análisis. 1983. No. 21 (May). Santiago: Sur Ediciones.

———. 1983. No. 22 (June) Santiago: Sur Ediciones.

———. 1983. No. 23 (July) Santiago: Sur Ediciones.

———. 1983. No. 24 (August) Santiago: Sur Ediciones.

———. 1984. No. 30 (March) Santiago: Sur Ediciones.

———. 1984. No. 32 (May) Santiago: Sur Ediciones.

———. 1984. No. 33 (June) Santiago: Sur Ediciones.

Hechter, M. 1987. *Principles of Group Solidarity*. Berkeley and Los Angeles: University of California Press.

Hersh, Seymour Martin. 1983. *The Price of Power: Kissinger in Nixon's White House*. New York: Summit Books.

Hertz Cadíz, Carmen. 1987. "Las ejecuciones políticas en Chile." presented at seminar on Justice and Human Rights in Santiago (January 11).

Hirschman, Albert. 1982. *Shifting Involvement: Private Interests and Public Action*. Princeton: Princeton University Press.

Hobsbawn, Eric J. 1959. *Primitive Rebels*. London and New York: W.W. Norton Co.

――――. 1978. "Should the Poor Organize?" *New York Review of Books* (March 28).

Hojman, David E. 1990. "Chile after Pinochet: Aylwin's Christian Democrat Economic Policies for the 1990's." *Bulletin of Latin American Research* 9, no. 1: 25–47.

Huneus, Carlos. 1987a. *Los Chilenos y la política: Cambio y continuidad en el autoritarismo*. Chile: Salesianos.

――――. 1987b. "From Diarchy to Polyarchy: Prospects for Democracy in Chile." In *Comparing Democracies: Transition and Consolidation in Mediterranean Europe and the Southern Cone*, ed. Enrique A. Baloyra, (Boulder, Colo.: Westview Press).

Huntington, Samuel P. 1968. *Political Order in Changing Societies*. New Haven: Yale University Press.

Informe de Encuesta. 1987. *Opinión publica y cultura política*. Santiago: CED/FLACSO.

Investor Responsibility Research Center. 1981. "United

States Corporate Activities in Chile." Proxy issue report. Washington D.C.: Investor Responsibility Research Center (March 18).

Jaquette, Jane S. ed. 1991. *The Women's Movement in Latin America: Feminism and the Transition to Democracy.* Boulder, Colo.: Westview Press.

Jenkins, J. Craig. 1979. "What Is To Be Done: Movement or Organization?" Review of *Poor Peoples Movements* by Francis Fox Piven and Richard Cloward. *Contemporary Sociology* 8, no. 2 (March): 222–228.

————. 1983. "Resource Mobilization Theory and the Study of Social Movements." *Annual Review of Sociology* 9: 552.

Jenkins, Craig J. and Charles Perrow. 1977. "Insurgency of the Powerless: Farm Worker Movements (1946–1972)." *American Sociological Review* 42: 249–268.

Katznelson, Ira. 1981. *City Trenches: Urban Politics and the Patterning of Class in the United States.* Chicago: University of Chicago Press.

Kaufman, Edy. 1988. *Crisis in Allende's Chile.* New York: Praeger.

Kaufman, Robert. 1976. "Transitions to Stable Authoritarian-Corporatist Regimes: The Chilean Case." *Sage Professional Papers in Comparative Politics* 5.

Kay, Cristobal and Patricio Silva. 1992. *Development and Social Change in the Chilean Countryside from the Pre-Land Reform Period to the Democratic Transition.* Amsterdam: Centro de Estudios y Documentación Latinoamericanos.

Keesing's Contemporary Archives. 1973–1985. Lynsham Bristol, Eng.: Keesing's Publications.

Klaarhamer, Raul. 1989. "The Chilean Squatter Movement and the State." In *Urban Social Movements and the State*, ed. Frans Schuurman and Ton van Naerssen. London and New York: Routledge.

Kusnetoff, Fernando. 1987. "Urban and Housing Policies under Chile's Military Dictatorship." *Urban Latin America*, ed. Robert Dash. *Latin American Perspectives* 14, no. 2 (Spring): 157–186.

Landsberger, Henry. 1968. "Do Ideological Differences Have Personal Correlates." *Economic Development and Cultural Change* 16, no. 2: 219–242.

Landsberger, Henry and Tim McDaniel. 1976. "Hypermobilization in Chile 1970–1973." *World Politics* 28, no. 4 (July).

Larraín, Cristián and Mario Velázquez. 1992. "Evolución económica 1990: Ajuste y mercado del trabajo." *Economía y trabajo en Chile: Informe anual* 46. Santiago: PET.

Larraín, Felipe B. 1991. "The Economic Challenges of Democratic Development." Pp. 276–303 in *The Struggle for Democracy in Chile 1982–1990*, ed. Paul W. Drake and Ivan Jaksic. Lincoln: University of Nebraska Press.

Latin American Economic Reports. 1977. "Chile's Economy Rocked by a Surfeit of Freedom" (January).

———. 1977. "Chile Returns to Favor with Foreign Bankers" (July).

————. 1977. "Chile Cuts Back Severely in Nationalized Sector" (November).

————. 1978. "Chile's New Economic Order Goes into the Constitution" (December).

————. 1979 "Timber Emerges as Export Growth Sector in Chile" (June).

————. 1979. "Chile's New Laws 'A Death Blow to Marxism'" (July).

————. 1980. "Mapping the Divide Between Rich and Poor" (December).

————. 1982. "An Ebbing Tide of Support Leaves the President in Shallow Water" (May).

————. 1983. "Chilean Regime Encouraged by 1977 Performance" (February).

Lawner, Miguel. 1987. Interview by author. Santiago (January).

Lechner, Norbert, ed. 1990. *Cultura política y democratización.* Santiago: FLACSO.

Leeds, Anthony and Elizabeth Leeds. 1976. "Accounting for Behavioral Differences: Three Political Systems and the Response of Squatters in Brazil, Peru, and Chile." Pp. 193–248 in *The City in Comparative Perspective,* ed. John Walton and Louis Masotti. Newbury Calif.: Sage Publications.

Leiva, Fernando Ignacio and James Petras. 1986. "Chile's Poor in the Struggle for Democracy." *Chile's Poor in the Struggle for Democracy, Rural Issues in Ecuador and Mexico,* ed. Robert Dash and Michael Kearney. Issue 51 of *Latin American Perspectives* 13, no. 4: 5–23.

Levy, Daniel C. 1986. "Chilean Universities under the Junta: Regime and Policy." *Latin American Research Review* 21, no. 3.

Linz, Juan and Alfred Stepan. 1992. "Political Identities and Electoral Sequences: Spain, the Soviet Union, and Yugoslavia." *Daedalus*, 121, no. 2 (Spring).

Lira, Elizabeth, and María Isabel Castillo. 1991. *Psicología de la amenaza política y del miedo*. Santiago: Instituto Latinoamericano de Salud Mental y Derechos Humanos (ILAS).

Loveman, Brian. 1993. "The Political Left in Chile, 1973–1990." In *The Latin American Left: From the Fall of Allende to Perestroika*, ed. Barry Carr and Steve Ellner. Boulder, Colo.: Westview Press and London: Latin American Bureau.

Lozza, Arturo M. 1986. *Chile sublevado: Reportaje del Frente Patriótico Manuel Rodríguez*. Lima: Ediciones Unidad.

Lukes, Steven. 1974. *Power: A Radical View*. London: MacMillan.

Mainwaring, Scott. 1987. "Urban Popular Movements, Identity, and Democratization in Brazil." *Comparative Political Studies* 20, no. 2: 131–159.

Malloy, James M. and Mitchell A. Seligson, eds. 1987. *Authoritarians and Democrats: Regime Transition in Latin America*. Pittsburgh: University of Pittsburgh Press.

Mangin, William. 1967. "Latin American Squatter Settlements: A Problem and a Solution." *Latin American Research Review* 2. (Summer): 65–98.

Maravall, Jose. 1978. *Dictatorship and Political Dissent*. London: Tavistock.

Martínez, Javier and Eugenio Tironi. 1985. *Las clases sociales en Chile: Cambio y estratificación, 1970–1980*. Santiago: Ediciones Sur.

McAdam, Doug. 1982. *Political Processes and the Development of Black Insurgency, 1930–1970*. Chicago: University of Chicago Press.

————. 1983. "Tactical Innovation and the Pace of Insurgency." *American Sociological Review* 48: 735–54.

Melucci, Alberto, 1988. "Getting Involved: Identity and Mobilization in Social Movements," Pp. 329–48 in *From Structure to Action: Comparing Movement Research across Cultures, International Social Movement Research*, ed. B. Klandermans, H. Kriese, and S. Tarrow, vol. 1. Greenwich, Conn.: JAI Press.

Millio, Boris. 1986. Interview by author. Santiago (October). Millio is a research associate at Servicio de Paz y Justicia.

Monckeberg, María Oliva and Alicia Oliva Juanitarojas. 1986. "Así fue el paro" *Análisis* (July 7–13).

Monteon, Michael. 1982. *Chile in the Nitrate Era: The Evolution of Economic Dependence 1880–1930*. Madison: University of Wisconsin Press.

Morales, Eduardo and Sergio Rojas. 1987. "Relocalización socioespacial de la pobreza: Política estatal y presión popular, 1979–1985." In *Espacio y poder: Los pobladores*, ed. Jorge Chateau et al. Santiago: FLACSO.

Morris, Aldon D. 1984. *The Origins of the Civil Rights*

Movement: Black Communities Organizing for Change. New York: Free Press.

———. 1992. "Political Consciousness and Collective Action." Pp. 351–375 in *Frontiers in Social Movement Theory,* ed. Aldon D. Morris and Carol McClurg. New Haven: Yale University Press.

Morris, Aldon D. and Carol McClurg Mueller, eds. 1992. *Frontiers in Social Movement Theory.* New Haven: Yale University Press.

Morris, James O. 1966. *Elites, Intellectuals, and Consensus: A Study of the Social Question and the Industrial Relations System in Chile.* Ithaca, N.Y.: Cornell University School of Industrial Labor Relations.

Moulian, Tomás. 1983. *Democracia y socialismo en Chile.* Santiago: FLACSO.

Munck, Gerardo L. 1994. "Authoritarianism, Modernization, and Democracy in Chile." *Latin American Research Review* 29, no. 2.

Neier, Aryeh and Cynthia Brown. 1987. "Pinochet's Way." *New York Review of Books* (June 25).

Nelson, Joan M. 1979. *Access to Power: Politics and the Urban Poor in Developing Nations.* Princeton: Princeton University Press.

Neruda, Pablo. 1976. *Memoirs,* translated from the Spanish *Confieso que he vivido: Memorias,* by the Estate of Pablo Neruda. New York: McGraw Hill.

Neruda, Pablo. 1978. *Passions and Impressions,* translated

from the Spanish, *Para nacer he nacido* by the Estate of
Pablo Neruda. New York: McGraw Hill.

Obershall, Anthony. 1973. *Social Conflict and Social Movements*. Englewood Cliffs: Prentice Hall.

O'Brian, Phil and Jackie Roddick. 1983. *Chile: The Pinochet Decade*. London: Latin American Bureau.

O'Donnell, Guillermo. 1978. "Tensions in the Bureaucratic Authoritarian State and the Question of Democracy." In *The New Authoritarianism in Latin America*, ed. David Collier. Princeton: Princeton University Press.

O'Donnell, Guillermo; Philippe C. Schmitter; and Laurence Whitehead, eds. 1986. *Southern Europe*, vol. 1 of *Transitions from Authoritarian Rule*. Baltimore: John Hopkins University Press.

————. 1986 *Latin America*, vol. 2 of *Transitions from Authoritarian Rule*. Baltimore: John Hopkins University Press.

————. 1986 *Comparative Perspectives*, vol. 3 of *Transitions from Authoritarian Rule*. Baltimore: John Hopkins University Press.

————. 1986 *Tentative Conclusions*, vol. 4 of *Transitions from Authoritarian Rule*. Baltimore: John Hopkins University Press.

O'Keefe, Tomas. 1986. "The Use of the Military Justice System to Try Civilians in Chile." unpublished article by an American lawyer who worked in the Chilean Commission of Human Rights and the Chilean Vicaria de Solidaridad.

Olson, Mancur. 1971. *The Logic of Collective Action: Public*

Goods and the Theory of Groups. Cambridge: Harvard University Press.

Oppenheim, Lois, ed. 1991. *Military Rule and the Struggle for Democracy in Chile.* Issue 68 of *Latin American Perspectives* 18, no. 1 (Winter).

————. 1993. *Politics in Chile: Democracy, Authoritarianism, and the Search for Development.* Boulder, Colo.: Westview Press.

Ortega Eugenio and Ernesto Tironi. 1988. *Pobreza en Chile.* Santiago: CED.

Oxhorn, Philip. 1986. "Democracia y participación popular: Organizaciones poblacionales en la futura democracia Chilena." No. 44 December Santiago: FLACSO.

————. 1991. "The Popular Sector Response to an Authoritarian Regime: Shantytown Organizations since the Military Coup." *Military Rule and the Struggle for Democracy in Chile,* ed. Lois Oppenheim. Issue 68 of *Latin American Perspectives* 18, no. 1 (Winter): 66–91.

Paley, Julia. 1994. *Knowledge and Urban Social Movements in Post-Dictatorship Chile.* Ph.D. diss., Department of Anthropology, Harvard University.

Panebianco, Angelo. 1992. *Political Parties: Organization and Power.* Cambridge: Cambridge University Press.

Pastrana, Ernesto and Monica Threlfall. 1974. *Pan, techo, y poder: El movimiento de pobladores en Chile (1970–1973).* Buenos Aires: Ediciones Siap-Planteos.

Perlman, Janice. 1976. *The Myth of Marginality: Urban*

Poverty and Politics in Río de Janeiro. Berkeley and Los Angeles: University of California Press.

Pinto, Anibal. 1984. "Metropolización y terciarización: Malformaciones estructurales." *Revista de la Comisión Económica para América Latina de Naciones Unidas* (CEPAL) 24. Santiago.

Piven, Frances Fox and Richard A. Cloward. 1979. *Poor People's Movements: Why They Succeed, How They Fail.* New York: Vintage.

Pizzorno, Alessandro. 1978. "Political Exchange and Collective Identity in Industrial Conflict." In *The Resurgence of Class Conflict in Western Europe since 1968,* ed. Colin Crouch and Alessandro Pizzorno, vol. 2. London: Macmillan.

———. 1993. "Some Other Kind of Otherness: A Critique of Rational Choice Theories." Unpublished paper.

Politzer, Patricia. 1988. *La ira de Pedro y los otros.* Santiago: Planeta Espejo de Chile.

Pollack, Benny and Hernan Rosencranz. 1980. *Revolutionary Social Democracy: The Chilean Socialist Party.* London: Frances Pinter.

Portes, Alejandro. 1969. "Cuatro poblaciones: Informe preliminar sobre situación y aspiraciones de Grupos Marginados en el Gran Santiago." Monograph Report. Santiago: University of Wisconsin Sociology of Development Program.

———. 1971. "Urbanization and Politics in Latin America." *Social Science Quarterly* 52 (December): 697–720.

————. 1972. "Rationality in the Slum." *Comparative Politics* 14, no. 3: 268–286.

————. 1976. "Occupation and Lower-Class Political Orientation in Chile." In *Chile: Politics and Society*, ed. Arturo Valenzuela and J. Samuel Valenzuela. New Brunswick, N.J.: Transaction Books.

————. 1985. "Latin American Class Structures: Their Composition and Change during the Last Decades." *Latin American Research Review* 20, no. 3: 7–39.

————. 1989. "Latin American Urbanization in the Years of the Crisis." *Latin American Research Review* 24, no. 3: 27–45.

————. 1993. Letter to the author (March 9).

Portes, Alejandro; Manuel Castells; and Laura Benton, eds. 1989. *The Informal Economy: Studies in Advanced and Less Developed Countries.* Baltimore: John Hopkins University Press.

Portes, Alejandro and Michael Johns. 1989. "The Polarization of Class and Space in the Contemporary Latin American City." In *The Informal Economy: Studies in Advanced and Less Developed Countries.* ed. Alejandro Portes, Manuel Castells, and Laura Benton. Baltimore and London: John Hopkins University Press.

Portes, Alejandro and John Walton. 1976. *Urban Latin America.* Austin: University of Texas Press.

Przeworski, Adam. 1985. *Capitalism and Social Democracy.* Cambridge: Cambridge University Press.

————. 1986. "Problems in the Study of Transitions to

Democracy." In *Comparative Perspectives*, vol. 2 of *Transitions from Authoritarian Rule*, ed. Guillermo O'Donnell, Philippe Schmitter, and Laurence Whitehead. Baltimore: John Hopkins University Press.

Putnam, Robert. 1993. *Making Democracy Work: Civic Traditions in Modern Italy*. Princeton: Princeton University Press.

Raczynski, Dagmar. 1988. "Crisis y urbanización en el área metropolitana de Santiago de Chile." Paper presented at the Seminar on Latin American Urbanization during the Crisis, Florida International University, Miami (January).

Razeto, Luis, et al. 1983. *Las organizaciones económicas populares*. Santiago: PET.

Reinoso, Luis. 1946. "La solución a los problemas nacionales a través de la enseñanzas del XIII Congreso." *Principios* 56–57 (February–March): 15–19. Cited by María Soledad Gómez in *El Partido Comunista ed Chile*, ed. Augusto Varas. Santiago: FLACSO, 89.

Remmer, Karen. 1991. *Military Rule in Latin America*. Boulder, Colo.: Westview Press.

Rivas, Gonzalo. 1992. "Esperanzas, logros, e inquietudes." *Economía y trabajo en Chile: Informe anual 46*. Santiago: PET.

Rivas, Gonzalo, et al. 1992. *Economía y trabajo en Chile: Informe anual 46*. Santiago: PET.

Roberts, Kenneth Morgan. 1992. *In Search of a New Identity: Dictatorship, Democracy, and the Evolution of the Left in Chile and Peru*. Ph.D. diss., Department of Political Science, Stanford University.

Rodríguez, Alfredo. 1983. *Por una ciudad democrática.* Santiago: Ediciones Sur.

Rodríguez, Alfredo and Eugenio Tironi. 1986. *Encuesta a pobladores de Santiago: Principales resultados* (December). Santiago: Ediciones Sur.

Rojas, Carmen. 1986. *Recuerdos de una Mirista.* Santiago: Antonia Gómez.

Rouquie, Alain. 1986. "Demilitarization and Military-Dominated Politics in Latin America." In *Comparative Perspectives,* vol. 3 of *Transitions from Authoritarian Rule,* ed. Guillermo O'Donnell, Philippe Schmitter, and Laurence Whitehead. Baltimore: John Hopkins University Press.

Rozas, Patricio, and Gustavo Marín. 1988. *El mapa de la extrema riqueza: Diez años después.* Santiago: CES.

Rueschemeyer, Dietrich; Evelyne Huber Stephens; and John Stephens. 1992. *Capitalist Development and Democracy.* Chicago: University of Chicago Press.

Ruiz-Tagle, Jaime. 1985. *El sindicalismo Chileno después del Plan Laboral,* Santiago: PET.

———. 1992. "Las Políticas Sociales en 1990–91." In *Economía y trabajo en Chile: Informe anual 46.* Santiago: PET.

Ruiz-Tagle, Jaime and Roberto Urmenta. 1984. *Los trabajadores del programa del empleo mínimo,* Santiago: PET.

Rule, James B. 1988. *Theories of Civil Violence.* Berkeley and Los Angeles: University of California Press.

Sabatini, F. 1982. "Santiago: Sistemas de producción de vivienda, renta de la tierra, y segregación urbana." Documento de trabajo 128. Santiago: Centro de Investigación y Docencia Urbana (CIDU–IPU) (April).

Sabia, Daniel R. Jr. 1988. "Rationality, Collective Action, and Karl Marx." *American Journal of Political Science* 32, no. 1 (February).

Salazar, Gabriel. 1990. *Violencia política popular en las grandes alamedas*. Santiago: Ediciones Sur.

Salimovich, Sofia; Elizabeth Lira; and Eugenia Weinstein. 1992. "Victims of Fear: The Social Psychology of Repression." In *Fear at the Edge: State Terror and Resistance in Latin America*, ed. Juan E. Corradi, Patricia Weiss Fagen, and Manuel Antonio Garretón. Berkeley and Los Angeles: University of California Press.

Santos, José Manuel. 1976. "La seguridad nacional, condición del bien común," September 18, *Mensaje* (Valdivia, Chile) 25 (November).

Sassoon, Anne Showstack. 1987. *Gramsci's Politics*. Minneapolis: University of Minnesota Press.

Schamis, Hector E. 1987. "From Bureaucratic Authoritarianism to Neoconservatism: Reassessing the Military Regimes of the Southern Cone in the 1970s." New York: Institute of Latin American and Iberian Studies, Columbia University.

Schild, Veronica. 1989. *Gender, Class, and Politics: Poor Neighborhood Organizing in Authoritarian Chile*, Ph.D. diss., Department of Political Science, York University.

Schkolnik, Mariana. 1986. *Sobrevivir en la población José María Caro y en Lo Hermida*, Santiago: PET.

Schneider, Cathy. 1989. *The Mobilization at the Grassroots: Shantytowns and Resistance in Authoritarian Chile*. Ph.D. diss., Department of Government, Cornell University.

————. 1990 "La movilización de las bases: Población es marginales y resistencia en Chile autoritario." Pp. 223–243 in *Chile historia y "bajo pueblo,"* ed. Gabriel Salazar, *Proposiciones* 19. Santiago: Ediciones Sur, (August).

————. 1991. "Mobilization at the Grassroots: Shanty-town Resistance in Authoritarian Chile." *Military Rule and the Struggle for Democracy in Chile*, ed. Lois Oppenheim. Issue 68 of *Latin American Perspectives* 18, no. 1 (Winter): 92–112.

————. 1992. "Radical Opposition Parties and Squatters Movements in Pinochet's Chile." Pp. 260–275 in *The Making of Social Movements in Latin America: Identity, Strategy, and Democracy*, ed. Arturo Escobar and Sonia E. Alvarez. Boulder, Colo.: Westview Press.

————. 1993. "Chile: The Underside of the Miracle." *North American Congress on Latin America Report on the Americas: A Market Solution for the Americas?: The Rise of Wealth and Poverty*. 26, no. 4 (February).

Scott, James C. 1985. *Weapons of the Weak*. New Haven: Yale University Press.

————. 1990. *Domination and the Arts of Resistance: Hidden Transcripts*. New Haven: Yale University Press.

Serrano, Bruno. 1986. *Los relegados de Lo Hermida.* Santiago: Ediciones Warriafilla.

Sheahan, John. 1987. *Patterns of Development in Latin America: Poverty Repression and Economic Strategy.* Princeton: Princeton University Press.

Sherman, Rachel. 1991. "Collective Actors and Political Systems: The Influence of Political Conditions on Neighborhood and Women's Movements in Brazil and Chile." Senior thesis in Development Studies, Brown University.

Shorter, Edward and Charles Tilly. 1974. *Strikes in France, 1830–1968.* New York: Cambridge University Press.

Silva, Patricio. 1991. "The Military Regime and Restructuring of Land Tenure." *Military Rule and the Struggle for Democracy in Chile*, ed. Lois Oppenheim. Issue 68 of *Latin American Perspectives* 18, no. 1 (Winter): 15–32.

Smith, Brian H. 1982. *The Church and Politics in Chile: Challenges to Modern Catholicism.* Princeton: Princeton University Press.

Smith, Carol, ed. 1990. *Guatemalan Indians and the State.* Austin: University of Texas Press.

Smith, William C.; Carlos H. Acuña; and Eduardo A. Gamarra, eds. 1994. *Democracy, Markets, and Structural Reform in Latin America: Argentina, Bolivia, Brazil, Chile, and Mexico.* New Brunswick, N.J.: Transaction Books.

Stallings, Barbara. 1979. *Class Conflict and Economic Development in Chile, 1958–1973.* Stanford: Stanford University Press.

Stepan, Alfred. 1971. *The Military in Politics: Changing Patterns in Brazil*. Princeton: Princeton University Press.

———. 1979. *The State and Society: Peru in Comparative Perspective*. Princeton: Princeton University Press.

———. 1985. "State Power and the Strength of Civil Society in the Southern Cone of Latin America." In *Bringing the State Back In*, ed. Peter Evans, Dietrich Rueschemeyer, and Theda Skocpol. New York: Cambridge University Press.

———. 1986. "Paths toward Redemocratization." In *Comparative Perspectives*, vol. 3 of *Transitions from Authoritarian Rule*, ed. Guillermo O'Donnell, Philippe Shmitter, and Lawrence Whitehead. Baltimore: John Hopkins University Press.

———. 1988a. "Chile and the Plebiscite," presented at Columbia University (October 19).

———. 1988b. "The Last Days of Pinochet?" *New York Review of Books* (May 9).

———. 1988c. *Rethinking Military Politics: Brazil and the Southern Cone*. Princeton: Princeton University Press.

Sullivan, Mercer. 1989. *Getting Paid: Youth, Crime, and Work in the Inner City*. Ithaca, N.Y.: Cornell University Press.

Tarrow, Sidney. 1967. *Peasant Communism in Southern Italy*. New Haven: Yale University Press.

———. 1989a. *Democracy and Disorder: Protest and Politics*

in Italy, 1965–1975. New York: Oxford University Press.

————. 1989b. *Struggle, Politics, and Reform: Collective Action, Social Movements, and Cycles of Protest,* Ithaca, N.Y.: Cornell University. Western Societies Paper no. 21.

————. 1992a. "Eastern European Social Movements: Globalization, Difference, and Political Opportunity?" Unpublished paper, prepared for presentation at the First European Conference on Social Movements, Berlin (October 29–31).

————. 1992b. "Mentalities, Political Cultures, and Collective Action Frames: Constructing Meanings through Action." Pp. 174–203 in *Frontiers in Social Movement Theory,* ed. Aldon D. Morris and Carol McClurg Mueller. New Haven: Yale University Press.

————. 1994. *Power in Movement: Social Movements, Collective Action, and Politics.* Cambridge: Cambridge University Press.

Teitelboim, Berta. 1987. "Indicadores económicos y sociales y series anuales, 1960–1986." *Serie de indicadores económico sociales.* Santiago: PET/Academia de Humanismo Cristiano (September).

Tilly, Charles. 1969. "Community: City: Urbanization." Mimeographed. Ann Arbor: University of Michigan.

————. 1978. *From Mobilization to Revolution.* Reading, Mass.: Addison-Wesley.

————. 1983. "Does Modernization Breed Revolution?" *Comparative Politics* 15, no. 3 (April).

————. 1993. Contentious Repertoires in Great Britain, 1758–1834, *Social Science History* 17, no. 2 (Summer).

Tilly, Charles; Louise Tilly; and Richard Tilly. 1975. *The Rebellious Century (1830–1930)*. Cambridge: Harvard University Press.

Timerman, Jacobo. 1987. *Chile: Death in the South*. New York: Alfred A. Knopf.

Tironi, Eugenio. 1984. *La Torre de Babel: Ensayos de critica y renovación política*. Santiago: Ediciones Sur.

————. 1987. "Pobladores e integración social." In *Marginalidad, movimientos sociales, y democracia*, ed. José Bengoa, Javier Martínez, and Eugenio Tironi, *Proposiciones* 14. Santiago: Ediciones Sur.

————. 1990. *Autoritarismo, modernización, y marginalidad*. Santiago: Ediciones Sur.

Tucker, Robert, ed. 1975. *The Lenin Anthology*. Princeton: Princeton University Press.

————. 1978. *The Marx-Engels Reader*. New York: W.W. Norton.

United States Senate Select Committee Intelligence. 1975. Staff Report. *Covert Action in Chile, 1963–1973*. Washington D.C.

Universidad de Chile. 1986. *Ocupación y desocupación: Encuestas nacional (1970–1985)*. Personal printout. Santiago: Departamento de Economía, Universidad de Chile.

Urrutia, Cecilia. 1972. *Historia de las es callampas, colección:*

Nosotros los Chilenos. Santiago: Serie: Hoy Contamos, Empresa Editora Nacional Quimantu Limitada.

Valdés, Teresa. 1982. "Poblaciones y pobladores: Notas para una discusión conceptual." *Materia de discusión*. No. 33. Santiago: FLACSO.

————. 1987. "El movimiento de pobladores, 1973–1985: La recomposición de las solidaridades sociales." In *Descentralización del estado: Movimiento social y gestión local*, ed. Jordi Borga et al. Santiago: FLACSO.

————. 1988. *Venid, benditas de mi padre: Las pobladoras, sus rutinas y sus sueños*. Santiago: FLACSO.

Valenzuela, Andrés. 1985. "Confesiones de un agente de seguridad." Interview by Monica González in *Cauce* (July 23–29).

Valenzuela, Arturo. 1978. *The Breakdown of Democratic Regimes: Chile*. Baltimore: John Hopkins University Press.

Valenzuela, Arturo and J. Samuel Valenzuela. 1986a. "Party Oppositions under Authoritarian Regimes." In *Military Rule in Chile*, ed. Arturo Valenzuela and J. Samuel Valenzuela. Baltimore: John Hopkins University Press.

————, eds. 1986b. *Military Rule in Chile*. Baltimore: John Hopkins University Press.

Valenzuela, Eduardo. 1984. *La rebelión de los jóvenes*. Santiago: Ediciones Sur.

————, ed. 1991. *Nacional Populismo, Voto Cambiante, Centro Político, Empleo Precario, Pequeño Empresariado, Identidad Cultural, Biotecnología*, ed. Eduardo Valenzuela, *Proposiciones* 20. Santiago: Ediciones Sur.

Valenzuela, J. Samuel. 1979. "Labor Movement Formation and Politics: The Chilean and French Cases in Comparative Perspective." Ph.D. diss., Department of Sociology, Columbia University.

Valenzuela, J. Samuel and Jeffrey Goodwin. 1983. *Labor Movements under Authoritarian Regimes*. Monographs on Europe, Center for European Studies, Harvard University.

Valenzuela, María Elena. 1981. *Todas íbamos a ser reinas: La mujer en el Chile militar*. Santiago: CES.

————. 1991. "The Evolving Role of Women." Pp.161–187 in *The Struggle for Democracy in Chile 1982–1990*, ed. Paul W. Drake and Ivan Jaksic. Lincoln: University of Nebraska Press.

Vanderschueren, Franz. 1971. "Significado político de las juntas de vecinos en las poblaciones de Santiago." *Revista Latinoamericana de estudios urbanos regionales* 2 (June): 67–90.

Van Hemelyryck, Librecht. 1991. "El desarrollo de la pequeña y microempresa en Chile: Un Desafío para el Futuro." Pp. 143–177 in *Nacional Populismo, Voto Cambiante, Centro Político, Empleo Precario, Pequeño Empresariado, Identidad Cultural, Biotecnología*, ed. Eduardo Valenzuela, *Proposiciones* 20. Santiago: Ediciones Sur.

Varas, Augusto. 1984. "Militarización y defensa nacional en Chile." *Mensaje* (June).

————. 1988. *El Partido Comunista en Chile*. Santiago: FLACSO.

Vega, Humberto. 1986. "Política económica y movimiento

laboral: Balance del ano 1985 y perspectivas para los anos 1986 y 1987." Santiago: PET.

Vergara, Pilar. 1990. *Políticas hacia la extrema pobreza en Chile, 1973–1988*. Santiago: FLACSO.

———. 1992. "Market Economy, Social Welfare, and Democratic Consolidation in Chile." Pp. 217–236 in *Democracy, Markets, and Structural Reform in Latin America: Argentina, Bolivia, Brazil, Chile, and Mexico*. ed. William C. Smith, Carlos H. Acuña, and Eduardo A. Gamarra. New Brunswick, N.J.: Transaction Books.

Vial, Gonzalo. 1981. *Historia de Chile*. Santiago: Editorial Portada.

Volk, Steven. 1983. "The Lessons and Legacy of a Dark Decade." *North American Congress on Latin America, Report on the Americas: Chile Beyond the Darkest Decade* 17, no. 5 (September/October).

Walker, Ignacio. 1986. Del populismo al Leninismo y la inevitabilidad del conflicto: El Partido Socialista de Chile (1933–1973). Notas técnicas 91. Santiago: Corporación de Investigaciones Económicas para América Latina.

Waugh, Michael S. 1992. "Depoliticization in Post-Pinochet Chile: Evidence and Implicaitons for Democratic Consolidation." Unpublished paper presented at Latin American Studies Association Conference, Los Angeles (September 24–27).

Weinstein Eugenia; Elizabeth Lira; and Eugenia Rojas, eds. 1987. *Trauma, duelo, y reparación*. Santiago: Fasic/ Interamericana.

Weinstein, José. 1991. "Victimas y beneficiarios de la modernización: Inventario de cambios el la juventud pobladora 1965–1990." *Nacional Populismo, Voto Cambiante, Centro Político, Empleo Precario, Pequeño Empresariado, Identidad Cultural, Biotecnología,* ed. Eduardo Valenzuela, *Proposiciones* 20. Santiago: Ediciones Sur.

Weinstein, Martin. 1988. *Uruguay: Democracy at the Crossroads.* Boulder, Colo.: Westview Press.

Wellman, Barry. 1979. "The Community Question: The Intimate Networks of East Yorkers." *American Journal of Sociology* 84, no. 5: 1201–1231.

Wilson, James Q. 1973. *Political Organization.* New York: Basic Books.

Wilson, Sergio P. 1985. *El drama de las familias sin casa y los allegados.* Santiago: Agrupación Vecinal.

Winn, Peter. 1986. *Weavers of Revolution: The Yarur Workers and Chile's Road to Socialism.* New York: Oxford University Press.

Zaslavsky, Victor. 1992. "Nationalism and Democratic Transition in Postcommunist Societies." *Daedalus* 121, no. 2 (Spring).

Zolberg, Aristide R. 1972. "Moments of Madness." *Politics and Society* 2: 183–207.

INDEX